RACISM AND
PAID WORK

# Racism and Paid Work

TANIA DAS GUPTA

Garamond Press

*To Esha Anum*

Typesetting and design: Robin Brass Studio
Printed and bound in Canada

Garamond Press
77 Mowat Ave., Suite 403
Toronto, ON
M6K 3E3

**Canadian Cataloguing in Publication Data**

Das Gupta, Tania, 1957-
      Racism and Paid Work

Includes bibliographical references and index.
ISBN 1-55193-000-5

1. Discrimination in employment. 2. Clothing
workers - Employment. 3. Nurses - Employment.
I. Title.

HD4903.D37 1996        331.13`3        C96-930267-3

The publication of this book has been supported by a grant from the Multiculturalism Program of the Department of Canadian Heritage. The opinions expressed do not necessarily reflect the views of the Government of Canada

# Contents

# Preface

THIS BOOK is a culmination of many years of activist and academic work which began soon after I came with my family to Canada. Being a woman of colour in this country, I was quickly aware of the entrenched relations of gender and racism that accompanies class oppression. I remember arguing for a feminist, anti-racist and Marxist standpoint in graduate school and having to struggle against the mainstream, even against Marxist or feminist scholars. Those were often very lonely and difficult days when I realized that I was marginalized even among "progressives".

Through that process, there are several individuals who supported me and continue to do so today. However, in most cases, they do not know the important role they have played in my intellectual development. Foremost among them are the many activists with whom I work(ed) in Toronto in support of women of colour, immigrant women, and South Asians communities: Salome Loucas, Diana Abraham, Christine Almeida, Akua Benjamin, Maria Wallis, Sabera Desai, the original group of women at the South Asian Women's Group (including my mother, Madhusree Das Gupta), Alexandra Cumsille, Pramila Aggarwal and Deena Ladd are some of the women who easily come to mind. My research and teaching reflect the many lessons, strategies and resources that I gathered by working with them. I also realized there *is* the possibility for social change.

I also need to acknowledge the late Dr. Madan L. Handa, my thesis supervisor and mentor, who supported my work consistently; the late Dr. Abdul Q. Lodhi who read my thesis and gave me the inspiration to move on when I had lost the motivation to do so; Dr. Roxana Ng for collaborating with me very early in my graduate studies; Mark Goodman for his warm encouragement and suggestion of designing a course on anti-racism at Atkinson College; my aunt, Dr. Joya Sen, who exposed me to progressive ideas and works very early on.

I would also like to thank the following members of my family for giving me unconditional love, encouragement, suppport and challenge: Amitabha Das Gupta, Madhusree Das Gupta, Tariq Saeed Kidwai, Dr. Bikram Das Gupta, Ishita Das Gupta, Esha Anum Kidwai, the late Pratip Kumar Das Gupta.

For this book specifically, I would like to acknowledge: Peter Saunders at Garamond Press for his immediate enthusiasm and encouragement; Hazelle Palmer for her excellent editorial suggestions; Cindy Wilkie, Jan Borowoy, Karen Lior, and Cynthia Enloe for reading various chapters and giving me their comments; and, to my colleagues at Atkinson College for supporting my sabbatical application during which this book was conceived and written. Finally, I would like to thank the many garment workers, nurses and people who work with them who shared with me their experiences, perceptions and insights.

Tania Das Gupta
Toronto, January 1996

# Chapter I

# Theoretical Framework:
# Class, Racism and Gender

## Introducing this Book

THIS BOOK explicitly addresses racism in paid workplaces in Canada. The case studies of the garment industry and of the nursing profession are based in Ontario. The province of Ontario has historically played a very significant role vis à vis the development of capitalism in the country; it has been part of an industrial heartland, and immigrants and people of colour, men and women alike, have played crucial roles in that developmental process. Demographically, about 60 per cent of immigrants settle in Ontario and most concentrate around Metropolitan Toronto. This region also has a significant proportion of people of colour in Canada. Linguistically, at least 60 per cent of the population of Toronto is of non-English or non-French background. Therefore, issues of diversity and "difference" have been part of the daily experiences, struggles and discourses of the populations in this region.

It is particularly timely to do a class, race and gender analysis of workplaces today as a number of local, national and international events have revealed the inter-relatedness of the rise of racism, sexism and classism within the "right-wing backlash." Internationally, the fall of the transitional socialist countries of Eastern Europe has discredited Marxist perspectives in many circles. In the post-NAFTA era, capital has become more and more flexible in crossing national boundaries, while at the same time nationalism in the form of "ethnic pride" and "ethnic cleansing" seems to be sweeping many societies. In Canada, the Reform Party has provided a political mouthpiece for anti-immigrant hysteria. In Ontario, a vigorously conservative government has undone overnight whatever

1

gains were made by the working class, women, and people of colour. In fact, it is now the poor, people of colour, women, and children who are scapegoats for the recession and who are further victimized in public in racist, sexist, and anti-poor discourses. These forces of conservatism are counteracted by popular organizing by women's associations, anti-racist coalitions, anti-poverty activists and the First Nations. This is the context in which this book was written.

I begin with an assumption of workplaces being located within a capitalist political economy where class relations and class struggle fundamentally shape the everyday lived relations of human beings. These lived relations are also shaped and mediated by racism, sexism and other forms of discrimination. It is difficult and pointless to identify the determinant relations in workplaces as there is a web of relationships based on class, gender, race, age, nationality and other socially constructed variables which are all inter-related and mutually reinforcing. I will discuss the rise of modern-day racism in the context of colonialism and slavery and the connections to the search for profit and cheap labour.

Capitalist establishments have particular historical tendencies, based on the profit motives of entrepreneurs. This requires minimizing costs. There are various ways in which capitalist workplaces and those in control accomplish this, depending on the nature of the industry and the socio-political context. Racism and sexism are handmaidens to this endeavour. Chapter one will elaborate on my theoretical framework. Following this, chapter two will discuss some of the daily manifestations of racism in workplaces. A case study of the garment industry is presented in chapter three and another on the nursing profession in chapter four. Finally, this book will conclude by providing information on the ways in which racism in paid workplaces has been resisted collectively and institutionally.

## Marxist Approach to the Labour Process

The approach of this book is Marxist, feminist and anti-racist. A Marxist approach entails a historical look of society, of social events, relationships or phenomena in order to lay bare underlying dynamics and tendencies which are at the root of everyday and "everynight"[1] realities. The determinant sphere of life according to the Marxist paradigm is in the production and reproduction of material existence, that is in the production of subsistence.[2] I want to extend this concept further by confirming what Burawoy[3] has said. People are not only producing things but also relations and ideas about those relations. Such ideas form part of the work environment and in most instances, reinforce social relations. However, they can be also contradictory in situations of worker resistance when workers articulate ideas that are contrary to dominant social relations.

One example of how workers reproduce hegemonic ideas can be found in garment industries. While the workers produce garments at the factories they are simultaneously confirming notions about women's roles as opposed to men's roles or what workers of Chinese heritage "are good at" for example, as opposed to Black workers, and so on. Managers and owners also take part in this process of reproducing ideas by consciously or unconsciously organizing particular divisions of labour based on racial, ethnic and gender stereotypes.

In the production of their means of subsistence, including ideas, people enter into relations with one another as individuals, as members of social classes and part of defined communities. The particular class relations in which people work are created by the nature in which surplus produced by workers – i.e., that part of the produce which is beyond what one needs for survival – is appropriated by the powerful class(es). Social power is the ability to affect other people's life chances through one's control over social resources, including human resources, and through one's position of privilege within the social hierarchies of racism, gender and class.

One of the inherent features of class societies is that of class struggle given that different classes and communities have various and opposing interests and aspirations. Thus, in capitalist societies, there is continuous struggle between the powerful classes and communities and those with less power and privilege. This has a profound impact on the organization of workplaces, including the selection of technologies, divisions of labour, choice of individual workers and, of course, on social relations overall. It also affects the balance of power between those with or without social power. Thus, to maintain an edge on power over workers and certain communities of workers, such as people of colour and women, owners and managers have evolved a variety of managerial techniques. Of course, even these techniques are conditioned by social relations and class struggle. Modes of control have proved to be more effective when they are established by a consensus of workers as opposed to coercion. Despite managerial techniques aimed at reducing class resistance, the coercion continues and takes different forms.[4]

Richard Edwards[5] has conducted a historical survey of the "control" methods or "management styles" that have been utilized in American workplaces from the nineteenth century to the 1970s. These range from personal, direct, and often coercive approaches, (e.g., physical and other forms of threats by management) to "technical" approaches which rely on technological innovation for control (e.g., mechanical monitoring systems and Taylorism), and finally to "bureaucratic" approaches which rule by impersonal laws (e.g., workers are obligated to satisfy standardized job descriptions, maintain company protocol, follow set career ladders and, follow accepted collective agreements).

Herman[6] has extended the discussion on control modes by connecting them to various industrial sectors. There are two modes of control in his analysis – dominative/coercive and hegemonic. The first is usually found in smaller, less mechanized establishments and the latter in larger, bureaucratic establishments. Hegemonic control modes are maintained by encouraging consensus among workers, for example by human relations' approaches and Quality of Work Life projects.

### Anti-Racist, Feminist Critiques

The problem with much of the Marxist discussions of labour processes and of paid work is that the working class is seen as a faceless, monolithic abstraction. This conception does not explain the different and contradictory experiences and responses of workers on the basis of such socially-defined features as gender and race. Their location within class relations as well as their experiences within similar positions are fundamentally conditioned by such features.

Canada is an advanced capitalist society where the owners and managers of business enterprises are the most powerful classes and those who do not own or control within these enterprises have less power. The development of capitalism in Canada and the complexities of its class structure is beyond the scope of this book and therefore will not be discussed here. However, what will be highlighted is that racism and gender are intrinsically woven into social relations, so that we begin to see workers, managers and owners as gendered and raced in addition to being classed.

Perhaps the most recent formal recognition of systemic discrimination in employment is contained in the Act to Provide for Employment Equity for Aboriginal People, People with Disabilities, Members of Racial Minorities and Women which became law in Ontario on September 1, 1994 under a New Democratic Party (NDP) government. The Preamble to the Bill recognized that the "target" communities experience higher rates of unemployment and more discrimination in job searches, in retaining employment and in being promoted. Therefore, these communities are under-represented in senior and management positions and over-represented in positions with low pay and little upward mobility. The lack of employment equity was recognized as being present in both the public and private sectors in Ontario.

The Canadian corporate elite is predominantly made up of White males. The boards of directors of Canada's major banks are predominantly White. Most corporations practice racial discrimination in hiring employees with collaboration from recruitment agencies.[7] Henry and Ginzberg's[8] study also documented that people of colour are under-represented in the trade and education/administration sectors and over-represented in the personal, health and welfare sectors. They are also under-represented in senior management and sales occupations and over-represented in general labour occupations. According to a 1990 report[9], only 4.1 per cent of executive positions in the Ontario Public Service were people of colour even though 11.8 per cent of all employees were from that community.

Workers are relegated to various positions within the division of labour in the same establishment and also between different sectors, depending on their sex and race. For instance, studies by Porter, Pineo and Mackie[10] concluded that peoples of colour, including Native Peoples, Asian and Black Canadians, were in subordinate positions in the occupational hierarchy.

Certain occupations have a minimal number of people of colour, such as in fire departments[11]. A 1985 McMaster University survey of 20 Canadian newspaper companies revealed that only 2 per cent of their employees were people of colour.[12] Metro Toronto Police which has had an employment equity program in place for several years had only 6 per cent people of colour on staff in 1990 in a metropolitan area with an estimated 20 per cent of its population being people of colour.[13] People of colour make up only 3.7 per cent of workers in the federal government.[14]

With the expansion of the state sector in the post-war era, many women found jobs in the clerical sector, although low-paid and of lower status compared to men. However, Sharma[15] discusses that these jobs were not accessible to women of colour due to racism.

## Labour Market Segmentation Theories

Theoretical works documenting sexual and racial segmentation within and between work sectors and workplaces have been limited. 'Dual market' and 'segmentation' theorists[16] argue that there are two separate labour markets – one being "primary" and the other being "secondary". The former includes an upper tier, sometimes referred to as an independent primary market, of professional and managerial workers with unionization, high pay and skills, status, and promotions. It also comprises a lower tier of middle-income groups, referred to as a subordinate primary labour market. The secondary labour sector is characterized by non-unionization, high labour turnover, different rules, and lower skill requirements. Edwards, Gordon and Reich[17] have connected these two labour markets with the "industrial core" and the "periphery." The former is dominated by larger, more capital-intensive and powerful firms. The latter is described as being a competitive sphere made up of many smaller companies, more labour intensive and less profitable, including small manufacturing and service industries. This sector would employ more women and Black and minority workers, whereas the industrial core would include more White and male workers.

## Critiques to Segmentation Theories

Many criticisms have been levelled at the dual labour market and related theorists. For instance, labelling smaller, more labour-intensive industries as peripheral to the economy has been rejected as inaccurate by feminist theorists. Gannage[18] argues that the garment industry, which is usually called peripheral, is the third largest manufacturing sector in Canada; it is a major employer of women and has been unionized since the 1900s. Moreover, the industry is marked by both highly-skilled workers as well as deskilled workers.

Some of these labour market segmentation theorists[19] have addressed the location of minority workers, people of colour and women workers, however they do not adequately account for the processes by which these groups end up in less secure, dead-end, low-paying jobs. In the absence of these elaborations, we are left with the assumption that women and people of colour are deficient and therefore are naturally suited to the less desirable work sectors. Also, dual labour market theorists do not account for differences among workers who have been lumped together, for instance between White women workers and women of colour, or between women and men of colour and, so on. How would they classify industrial homeworkers, that is, those who do piece work at home for contractors? Their conditions of work are far worse than for workers doing comparable work in factories or offices.

Reitz[20] assessed the job security level of selected ethnic groups, including Canadians of Chinese and Caribbean ancestry. The rankings, after adjustments due to inequalities in qualifications, revealed that Chinese-Canadian men and women and Caribbean-Canadian men were in the lowest positions compared to the other ethnic groups who happened to be White. Caribbean-Canadian women had a relatively high rank in terms of job security because of their higher unionization level, even though their incomes were the lowest among all the groups examined. The low incomes earned by Caribbean-Canadians are also confirmed by Henry and Tator[21] and Henry and Ginzberg.[22]

The Abella Commission Report[23] confirmed that the lowest incomes were earned by Black, Native, South-East Asian, and Central and South American peoples. The same report also documented high unemployment rates by Native Peoples, French-Canadians, South-East Asians, South Asian women and Black men.

A Census conducted in 1988 of federally-regulated organizations, including crown corporations covered under the Employment Equity Act, revealed that racial discrimination exists in hiring and that people of colour earn on average 7 per cent less than White workers.[24]

In 1995, women who worked full-time in Canada earned on average 72.0 per cent of what men earn. What was not reported is that women of colour earned only 51 per cent of what White men earned and 59 per cent of what men of colour earned.[25]

Working class immigrant women and women of colour are concentrated in four sectors of the labour market. First, they are present in relatively large numbers in processing and light manufacturing. [26]

Second, they are concentrated in the service sector, e.g., cleaning, cafeteria, restaurants and health. One-third of Metro Toronto's workers of colour are nursing attendants in homes for the aged. More than half are Black and 93 per cent are women.

Third, they are found in domestic work where women are brought under special contracts to perform duties for specific employers for limited time periods. They have no permanent immigration status in Canada. If their contracts are broken for any reason, these workers can be deported immediately. Some have likened the domestic program to the "indentured" system of labour.

The final sector where there are large numbers of women of colour and immigrant women is in the lower levels of large bureaucratic organizations in both the private and public sectors. For example, they are found in low-level clerical, secretarial and related occupations, as well as in the kitchen, housekeeping and laundry departments at hospitals. (Head, 1985).[27]

Dual labour market theorists also do not address the problematic definition of "skill" as a product of class struggle and intra-class struggle. Those workers who are better organized have been able to define their work as being "skilled" and hence the ones outside the bargaining fold are the "unskilled." Cockburn, Game and Pringle[28] have argued that male-dominated unions have defined jobs done by men as skilled even when their jobs were deskilled. I would hypothesize that jobs done by people of colour are also labelled as unskilled for the very same reason. It is not uncommon for people to refer to "immigrant workers" or to "immigrant women workers" as unskilled because they are relatively new in Canada and therefore do not have "Canadian experience," they do not speak one or other of the official languages, or their previous skills and qualifications have been devalued in Canada. In other words, their skill level is socially constructed by systemic forces of devaluation based on racism and xenophobia.

### Race and Gender Relations and Managerial Approaches

Managerial strategies also have a differential impact on workers of diverse ethnicity and gender. The modes of control depends on the type of workers available, e.g., their ethnicity and race, and also on how threatened management feels by these workers. For instance, even in a large, bureaucratic workplace, coercive modes usually associated with smaller workplaces might be utilized with workers of colour. For example, they may be arbitrarily fired on the subjective biases of a White supervisor without standard procedures being followed. At the same time, White workers may be managed by bureaucratic rules. These bureaucratic modes of control, which are apparently impersonal and standardized, can leave room for subjectivity and, thus, bias. For instance, we may find that even in bureaucracies, "subjectivity" plays a significant role in hiring decisions and in promotions. The requirement of formal training for specialized tasks and the inaccessibility of such training for most workers of colour are examples of bureaucratic control modes which adversely affect Black workers and workers of colour.

Another powerful control mechanism for management, particularly in large workplaces, is the heterogenization and segmentation of the workforce into racial stereotypes which emanate from the history of colonialism and slavery.[29] The solidarity of workers sometimes facilitated by ethnic, racial and gender homogeneity presents a potential threat to management. To counter this tendency, ideologies such as sexism and racism can be functional from management's perspective in facilitating worker segmentation. White workers and workers of colour, segregated by jobs, skill levels and physical space, serve to maintain their divided consciousness and power.

Management needs to maintain the powerlessness of all workers, but particularly of Black workers and workers of colour in order to maintain a division of labour based on race and ethnicity. This is accomplished by management practices which may be systemically biased against people of colour. Management may also use, consciously or unconsciously, differential treatment so that workers of colour are being "managed" and "disempowered" uniquely because they are seen as being fundamentally different from their White counterparts.

### Racism and Sexism as Ideologies and Economic Relations

From the very beginning there has been a connection between the capitalist economy and racism. Racism is one of the most hegemonic ideologies in Canadian society. The ideology rationalizes the differentiation and subordination of people on the basis of superficial physical characteristics, such as skin colour, or on some feature which can define a group or community as "different" from the "norm" of society. Sexism and classism are ideologies of/for discriminating between men and women and between social classes respectively. They are all constructed on the basis of physical, reproductive and social differences between individuals. In everyday living, these ideologies interact and influence each other, sometimes in complimentary ways and at other times in contradictory ways. For instance, working class women of colour and Black women are subordinated by an interplay of racist, sexist and classist ideologies.

In the Canadian context, people who have been subjected to racism are the Native Peoples, and Canadians of African, Caribbean, Asian, South American, Arab, Jewish and Moslem backgrounds. The social, economic and political context within which discrimination or racism is experienced also has a fundamental effect on the nature and scope of oppression. This book will focus mainly on anti-Black and anti-Chinese racism, particularly as they are manifested in paid work in the garment industry and in nursing.

### Attitudinal, Behavioural and Everyday Forms of Racism

Racist ideologies are manifested today in different forms, namely stereotypes and prejudices. They form the bases for individual and systemic acts of racism. Racial stereotypes refer to fixed ideas about people, usually based on insufficient or erroneous information about such people, their history and origins. Examples of stereotypes are the following: "Blacks are good basketball players", "Asians are passive", "Chinese are bad drivers." Racial prejudices refer to negative pre-judgements about people on the basis of stereotypes. For example, "Jews are greedy," "Native Peoples are lazy", "Blacks are criminal," are all prejudicial statements. Stereotypes and prejudices are both "attitudes" and they don't necessarily have to be accompanied by social power.

Attitudinal surveys conducted in Canada indicate various levels of racist attitudes in the population. One of the first of these surveys, conducted by Henry in 1978[30], revealed that the majority of Whites in Toronto held some degree of racist attitudes towards Blacks and South Asians. Nearly 16 per cent were "extremely racist" and another 33 per cent were "somewhat racist."

A survey conducted in 1991[31] revealed that many Canadians feel less comfortable with people of colour than they do with other groups. Fifteen percent felt that racial inter-marriage is a bad idea. Compared to an earlier survey conducted in 1974, attitudes towards minorities and racism seem to have improved. However, there are still significant numbers of people who feel negatively towards these issues. For instance, in 1991, 18 per cent of Canadians believed that a multiculturalism policy would destroy the Canadian way of life (32 per cent in 1974 felt similarly). Thirty-seven per cent in both 1991 and 1974 felt that a multiculturalism policy would cause greater conflict between different ethnic groups.

In a study titled *No Discrimination Here?* by Henry and Ginzberg[32], it was revealed that 51 per cent of management of 199 large companies (more than 50 employees) surveyed held negative views on people of colour. Twenty-eight per cent felt the latter do not have the ability to meet job performance requirements; 13 per cent perceived them as threatening, particularly if they gained promotions over Whites; 7 per cent expressed outright contempt for people of colour.

An audit of race relations in the Metro Toronto Police Force, revealed the development over time of stereotypes and prejudices about people of colour "which can and do produce a bias in behaviour which produces unequal treatment of individuals of different cultural or racial background."[33] Residents of the Jane-Finch community in Toronto have often voiced concerns about the "drug problem" being linked automatically by police and other mainstream institutions to "Jamaicans" and "Jamaican gangs."[34]

On the other hand, both individual and systemic racism are behaviours based on racist attitudes and are facilitated by social power. Therefore, class and/or gender privileges usually accompany an individual act of racism. Individual discrimination takes place when an individual with social power takes an action that has a derogatory effect on a person of colour. For example, a landlord denies an apartment to a Black person because he thinks that all Black people cause trouble. A White employer refuses to hire a South Asian at the managerial level because she feels that all South Asians, particularly women, are passive and therefore lack leadership skills.

Discriminatory jokes by a colleague in an office are also examples of individual discrimination. The office "comedian" may articulate something on the basis of his racist, sexist or classist attitudes. But, he is doing something else. He is actually verbalizing his discriminatory attitudes. A White office-worker who cracks racist, sexist or classist jokes presumably does so on the basis of his or her privilege within racial, gender or class relations. This can be referred to as "harassment", which occurs when someone in a position of social power is doing or saying something to make another person feel uncomfortable and unsafe.[35]

Research in Canada indicates that individual acts of racism occur frequently in workplaces. In three consecutive surveys conducted by the Canadian Civil Liberties Association[36] in 1975, 1980 and 1991, it was revealed that most employment agencies surveyed in Toronto would agree to discriminate in their referral of employees. Therefore, racist employers could utilize these agencies to suit their prejudices. Twelve out of 15 agencies surveyed agreed to comply with such requests from potential employers.

Systemic discrimination arises from conscious or unconscious policies, procedures and practices which adversely affect people of colour, such as their exclusion, marginalization and infantalization. Systemic discrimination is supported by institutional power, i.e., by the allocation of resources, codification of "standard" policies and procedures, and by workplace environment. Therefore, systemic racism is perpetuated over time. A good example of systemic racism, sometimes called "constructive" or "neutral rule" discrimination, is police department requirements which, until recently, had certain height and weight criteria for applicants. These criteria, in effect, excluded Asian Canadians and also women. These job requirements however, are now understood to be unnecessary "because strength and skills needed for police work are not primarily related to body size and height."[37]

A more complex example of systemic racism is an interview situation where a White, female interviewer from an Anglo-Saxon background feels and responds more positively to a candidate from the same background because she "gets a good feeling about this candidate." The interviewer shortlists this candidate for further interviews based on this "good feeling."

Systemic discrimination allows individuals to practice discrimination. In other words, when an individual with power can discriminate against people of colour within an institution without any checks, in the absence of complaints procedures or redress possibilities, then those discriminatory acts are being harboured systemically and institutionally. Those in power within the institution stand to gain from that situation.

A study of racism in the labour market by Henry and Ginzberg[38] revealed systemic racism in the recruitment, application and interview stages. Four teams, each consisting of a White and a Black candidate, with the same qualifications were sent to answer newspaper ads with similar résumés. The ads were from the retail food industry, retail sales, junior managerial positions and unskilled labour. In all, 201 jobs were applied for. White applicants received more application forms, encountered more helpful attitudes from potential employers, were more likely to be called for second interviews and were offered more jobs. On the basis of this controlled research, a 3:1 ratio of racial preference for jobs was determined. For every three job offers received by a White man, a Black man received one.

A comparison was also made of the treatment received over the phone by applicants with "minority ethnic" sounding names and with or without a non-dominant accent. Over half of the 237 employers contacted practiced some form of discrimination against one or more callers. South Asian callers experienced the most discrimination, followed by Caribbean people of African descent, followed by White immigrant callers.

Research conducted by the Ontario Human Rights Commission[39] pointed to a marked discrimination in the employment of people of colour. The latter are said to make more applications, and appear in more job interviews relative to Whites, but receive fewer offers. They receive less promotions and are only minimally present in managerial jobs. There were four times as many Whites in the latter positions as compared to people of colour.

Stereotypes, prejudices, individual discrimination and systemic discrimination are not mutually exclusive. In fact, they are mutually reinforcing. In other words, if there is systemic racism in a workplace, then chances are that individuals with power and authority in it are acting in ways that are adversely affecting people of colour. Moreover, these individuals with power and authority are acting on the basis of prejudices and stereotypes about people of colour.

At the level of everyday living, ideologies appear obvious and unproblematic. However, what becomes shared as "good" or "normal by society often has an adverse impact on a subgroup, such as people of colour. For example, consider a scenario where a White patient's relative walks into a hospital unit and asks the Black woman standing in front:

"Can I talk to someone in charge?" The Black woman was the nurse in charge in this scenario. The patient's relative was operating on the basis of a shared norm that a "person in charge" is inevitably a White man or woman because "Whiteness" is associated with leadership, responsibility, education and skill. Conversely, a Black woman is automatically assumed to be subordinate because "Blackness", especially combined with female-ness, is associated with inferiority and lack of responsibility.

The "everyday culture" of racism is systemic, subtle and common-place. A White person does not necessarily have to act consciously or "in a mean manner" in order to be racist. For example, workplace harassment does not necessarily have to be specifically directed at an individual in or-der for it to cause discomfort or adversity to that individual. *Environmen-tal racism*, sometimes referred to as a *poisoned environment*[40] can amount to racism or sexism. For instance, discriminatory jokes, graffiti and posters hung on the wall may not be specifically directed at *a* person of colour, but they may create an environment for that same person which nega-tively affects her mental well being and sense of safety, which in turn af-fects her efficiency. Racism is the *effect of* rather than the *intention to cause* deprivation to people of colour.[41]

Received traditions and practices, apparently seen as "fair" and "neu-tral", can amount to racism. The corollary to that, as Peggy McIntosh[42] has lucidly discussed, is *white privilege*. The latter is a set of interactions, relationships and experiences in everyday living which confers unearned advantages on White peoples. These advantages are unacknowledged, taken for granted and reproduced daily and generationally. Examples may include a White nurse being friendly with another nurse from her own racial background without feeling that she might be labelled as "sticking to her own kind." Another example is when a White professional gives some constructive feedback to her supervisor, she can do so without feel-ing that she might be labelled as being "aggressive" and "insubordinate." These are situations that White people would take for granted, while people of colour do not.

## Racism Preserves Cheap Labour and Powerlessness

Racism continues today as part of our everyday culture, and as a conven-ient ideology for maintaining cheap labour provided by people of colour and Black people. As industrial capitalism developed, the drive to increase profits and thus future investments led entrepreneurs and managers to seek out "cheaper" forms of labour. As mentioned, the ideology of racism has, in post-slavery and post-colonial days, still resulted in the over-representation of Black workers and workers of colour in the least desirable, least secure, poorest paid segments of the workforce. Simultaneously, they have been excluded from better paid, secure, more desirable jobs through systemic practices in the labour market and in other related institutions, such as the educational system.

The segregation of workers on the basis of racism into different work areas is based on and reinforced by common notions about "race", "racial difference" and "racial inequality." The labour of people of colour and of Black people is assumed to be "natural", "unskilled", and therefore inferior similar to the evaluation of women's labour. The labour of women of colour is evaluated in a doubly negative manner because it is based on an intertwining of racist and sexist ideologies. Hence, jobs done by people of colour are defined as being "less important" socially and thus of less value, justifying low status and therefore low wages. Stereotypical job allocations with undesirable working conditions are predicated on the powerlessness and vulnerability of workers of colour, including women. The assumption is that if workers of colour lack bargaining power, then the status quo can continue, to their disadvantage.

However, it is important to understand that not all Black workers and workers of colour are a part of the working class. Some theorists[43] have made the mistake of collapsing race into class, thereby assuming that people of colour and Black people are all in a most disadvantageous position within social relations. Even though there is a close connection between the two sets of relations, there are anomalies and they each have autonomous dynamics. Despite the systemic discrimination that is all-pervasive in society, some individuals of colour experience mobility and find themselves in middle- or upper-class locations. What is interesting is that these individuals still continue to suffer the indignities of racial and sexual discrimination. They continue to face barriers in the form of segregation in less desirable work, e.g., less desirable shifts and specializations, or being paid less than their White counterparts. They may find themselves as "tokens", that is, isolated, not having "real" authority, or being subjected to harassment.

Black professionals, such as doctors and lawyers experience racial and sexual discrimination.[44] According to Sparks,[45] Black lawyers in Canada seem to be channelled into certain areas of law, e.g., public interest and family law, and away from corporate and taxation law. They also seem to be streamed into certain types of law practice, e.g., government law and sole practice, rather than corporate counselling. Comparative research from Britain and the U.S. confirms this reality.[46] Racist and sexist hiring practices are evident as female lawyers of colour experience a great deal of difficulty becoming articled, and subsequently getting hired. There are few partnerships in judicial appointments and in professional associations. Sparks reports that female lawyers of colour are allocated work in a discriminatory manner, e.g., they are often made to run errands much like office secretaries are traditionally expected to do, or they are kept away from cases which deal with race or gender issues on the pretext that they may be biased in their handling. Their contributions are often trivialized and unrecognized by maintaining their invisibility to clients. Those with non-dominant accents are often not taken seriously by judges and clients, despite their skills as lawyers.

According to 1971 statistics, Chinese and Jewish-Canadians were the most highly educated in Canada,[47] however the former was 18th in terms of income, compared to the latter who were first. Reitz's study[48] confirmed that the Chinese male and female workers surveyed earned low incomes and experience low job security relative to their higher job status and higher qualifications. It is clear that class privilege does not shield people of colour from being subjected to racism and sexism.

## Anti-Black Racism

Anti-Black racism is an ideology directed towards individuals of African heritage and which began with slavery in Europe, tying together the histories of Europe, the Americas, the Caribbean and Africa. Since the 1400s, Portuguese sailors have attempted to capture Africans and sell them as house servants. This was given royal and papal blessings. Meanwhile, explorations of new trade routes were also sought by both the Portuguese and the Spanish with contacts made with India as well as South America and the Caribbean. Plantations and mining, which required cheap and large pools of labour, were forced onto the Native Peoples of these regions. In the process of colonization and settlement Native Peoples were, in most cases, subjected to violence, disease, destruction and death.[49] This is the context in which the African slave trade developed in the 1500s and continued until about 1807. Many Canadians do not realize that slavery existed in Canada until about 1783. The first slave landed in Quebec in 1628.

The overwhelming characteristics of the slave trade were the complete dehumanization of slaves and the sheer volume of the trade itself. Racist ideology developed in order to rationalize such mass cruelty and inhumanity. An ideology is a coherent set of ideas which provides an explanation of reality, but is typically a partial reality.[50] Hegemonic ideologies are those that have become dominant and accepted by most as being the best explanation of their reality and therefore in everyone's best interest to uphold. They have become part of our normative structure and, indeed, an aspect of everyday culture. As such, they are accepted by everyone unconsciously and uncritically. An important element of hegemony is the making of consensus among people who are subordinate within social relations. Ideologies become shared, learned and transmitted over generations.

As mentioned before, anti-Black racism is a direct extension of colonial and slave relations. According to those relations, a Black person was seen to be animal-like, less than human, having different abilities and skills due to inherent inferiority to Europeans. Therefore, their labour was also devalued. There were peculiar sexual mythologies around Black men and women, the latter seen to have an overwhelming reproductive capacity and the former lusting after White women.

There were also several contradictory images of Black women. On the one hand there was the slow, de-sexed, "cow-like" mammy, evolved into the "Aunt Jemima "figure, – familiar to many from older boxes of pancake mix – a servile and contented image which brings together gender and race ideologies. On the other hand, there was the sexual objectification of Black women's bodies, or body parts to be more exact.[51]

Davis,[52] Brand[53] and Thornhill[54] have all written on the legacies of slavery for Black women. Thornhill writes of the stereotype of Black women as "Amazon women enduring hardships, the likes of which no "lady" could endure" and the "tough, domineering, aggressive matriarch." Both of these stereotypical images are derived from the fact that under slavery Black women worked in physical, back-breaking work, similar to her male counterparts. She was beaten just as harshly and dehumanized like Black men. She was "nullified as Women."[55]

Under slavery, Black people could not maintain families on their own terms. Black women were regularly subjected to rape and other forms of sexual violence by White slave masters and they also had to bear their children. The slave masters decided on all marriages among his slaves and frequently decided on who would bear whose children. Slavery had no respect for family ties among Black people. Husbands, wives and children were separated arbitrarily. Thus, the rearing and supporting of children were left to women. The material and social conditions did not allow Black women to develop the attributes of upper class, European "femininity." Her role as a mother, as an enslaved person, as a builder of her community required her to be strong physically and mentally, to be a decision-maker and, in some cases, a leader.

Davis[56] writes that since Black women were oppressed equally, if not more severely, as Black men they resisted the oppression of slavery just as strongly. Thornhill[57] mentions the long list of African heads of state who were female and the latter day slave leaders such as Marie-Joseph-Angelique who set fire to her mistress' house in 1734 upon discovering that she would be sold the next day. There was also Harriet Tubman, a leader of the Underground Railroad, who led over 300 slaves from Southern U.S. to relative freedom in Canada. Davis[58] writes that the resistance to slavery that women displayed was a "terrifying revelation" for slave-owners who devised "especially brute repression" to punish them, including rape. This history has given rise to the stereotypes of Black women being "aggressive", "matriarchs", "Amazons" and "dangerous".

Hooks[59] writes that "radical" Black females even in modern times are often labelled as "crazy" by their opponents. This is a tactic used to silence women who are critical of the status quo and outspoken in their opposition to it. This tradition of organizing, leadership and outspokenness has given rise to the stereotype of Black women being "evil and treacherous".

The negative labels, sexist and racist stereotypes, are themselves indicative of a culture that does not see Black women in particular and people of colour in general as individuals, with their own identities and personalities. Instead, labels are imposed to create fixed images about entire communities based on their skin colour and other physical appearance. Hooks[60] argues that the "devaluation of Black womanhood" continued beyond slavery largely as a form of social control, i.e., to prevent their accomplishments since that would destroy White supremacist ideology.

Slavery-based stereotypes have been kept alive in a variety of ways. They are passed on through the educational system, most notably through the curriculum, including the hidden curriculum. This can happen by omission or by commission. The absence of images of Black people can perpetuate the impression that "they don't exist" and that "they are unimportant". When images such as photographs, illustrations, and cartoons, are included, they are often caricatures, portrayed in stereotypical roles, e.g., as helpers, as farmworkers and as manual labourers. Language can also be employed in biased ways so that popular stereotypes and prejudices are reinforced. For instance, by using phrases like "the darkest continent" in describing parts of Africa or saying it was a "dark day" when the stock market crashed, it equates "darkness" or "blackness" with negativity and evil and reinforces prejudices against Black people. Referring to Africans as "primitive" reinforces the stereotype of Black people being inferior. McDiarmid and Pratt[61] in a classic study evaluated 143 social studies texts from the Ontario Ministry of Education's list. Their conclusion was that textbook illustrations perpetuate stereotypes against Africans and Native Peoples as being naked, or half-naked, as fighting weapon in hand, as exotic, as subordinate, and so on. These conclusions have been confirmed by more current studies.

Popular culture in the form of visual media, print media, art, music, dress, forms of entertainment, sports, toys, games, etc. all perpetuate racist stereotypes and prejudices. Hooks[62] recognizes the connection of domination and representation. In order for anti-Black racism to continue, images and representations of Black people have to reinforce the stereotypes emanating from slavery. These images condition how non-Blacks will perceive Blacks, how they will interact with each other and how power will be distributed.

The power of ideology is such that even when slavery ended in the Americas, anti-Black racism survived. Black workers were still associated with dependence, suitable only for unskilled and service-oriented jobs.

The first post-slavery Black people to come to Halifax were the Black loyalists in 1783, who won their freedom by joining the British in the War of Independence. They were promised free land in New Brunswick and Nova Scotia. However, they were served after White loyalists, and therefore most received no land whatsoever. The few that did received sub-standard land which could hardly yield anything. Therefore, they had to support themselves by working as wage labourers in the homes and farms of White Canadians. Walker[63] describes the "caste-like" status of Blacks as they experienced economic dependence on White society and also segregation and marginalization in residential, church and educational lives.

The next group to come to Canada were refugees from the War of 1812, also fleeing slavery. Although they were somewhat welcomed in Canada, they were once again relegated to labouring and service jobs as had been their defined roles under slavery. Despite widespread discrimination, social segregation and poverty, Black Canadians cleared the land, established their own communities and built schools. However, their political vulnerability was driven home when Africville, a Black-Canadian settlement in Halifax, was bulldozed for industrial development. The Black community was not given any compensation whatsoever in return.[64]

The Black community is the only community of colour around which "riots" have taken place in current times. "Near riot" conditions on the streets of Halifax, Nova Scotia in July, 1991 were matched by similar outbursts in Montreal at the very same time and in Toronto in May, 1992. In all these instances, the violence was not isolated but rather indicative of racism in larger White society and the frustration of Black youth at being denied access and opportunities socially, economically and politically. Unemployment among Blacks in Nova Scotia is estimated to be as high as 80 per cent.[65]

In the aftermath of the "riot" in Halifax, a report was written by the Nova Scotia Advisory Group on Race Relations,[66] comprising representatives of three levels of government and of the Black community. The report notes that racism is part of the daily existence of Black people in Nova Scotia:

Black Nova Scotians still do not enjoy equal access to jobs; their businesses have difficulty succeeding because they do not have equal access to funding.... The educational system does not reflect their history and experience; the criminal justice system does not treat them fairly; they are often negatively portrayed in the media; and they cannot gain equal access to places of entertainment such as bars.[67]

A report by the Reference Group, made up of Black tenants and professionals who have lived in public housing in Metro Toronto released a report[68] which documented that Blacks are over-represented in 10 "high risk" projects of Metro Toronto Housing Authorities (MTHA), while MTHA's low-rises and bungalows are predominantly housing White tenants. This pattern has resulted in "ghetto-like" conditions, something that Canadians like to relegate only to the United States.

One report which is the most pointed in its discussion of anti-Black racism is that by Stephen Lewis[69], written in the aftermath of the May 1992 "Yonge Street riots" in Toronto. Lewis points out that it is the Black community that is shot at by police, streamed in schools, forced to "drop out", subjected to racism in MTHA facilities and being denied employment equity.

He mentions that many members of the Black community, particularly parents, live in fear of encounters with the police. This is because of the frequent shootings of Black youth by police.

In a Court of Appeal decision[70] involving Carlton Parks, (a Black male appellant convicted of manslaughter of a White male), Justice David Doherty discusses the reality of anti-Black racism in Canada and in particular in Metro Toronto. Stephen Lewis' conclusions discussed earlier are also reconfirmed by Doherty. He says:

> I do not pretend to essay a detailed critical analysis...however, I must accept the broad conclusions repeatedly expressed in these materials. Racism, and in particular anti-Black racism, is a part of our community psyche. A significant segment of our community holds overtly racist views. A much larger segment subconsciously operates on the basis of negative racial stereotypes....[71]

The decision mentioned that the Commission on Race Relations in the Criminal Justice System was formed as one of the results of the Stephen Lewis Report, and its focus is anti-Black racism in urban centres. Justice Doherty ruled that the conviction of the appellant was to be quashed because his lawyer had been prevented by the trial judge from asking potential jurors about their ability to be impartial, given that the accused is Black and the victim is White.

The Commission on Race Relations in the Criminal Justice System[72] has issued an interim report. The commission's findings confirm the indications of anti-Black racism, particularly in the prevalence of hostile prison environments and racial segregation in Ontario prisons. Research revealed that overtly racist language, i.e., name calling, racial stereotyping of Black prisoners and staff, and excessive use of force against Black prisoners are common practices. Racial stereotypes such as Black people being stupid, noisy, aggressive, violent, disorderly and Black women being immoral, promiscuous and sexually unstable are common in prisons. One senior prison administrator said that "Black people are feared, considered dangerous."[73] Jamaican-Canadians are particularly targeted for racial harassment and Blacks are often stereotyped as being "Jamaicans."

Many Black prisoners reported that correctional officers' (C.O.) behaviour towards them was often guided by their stereotypes of Black people. If Black people act in stereotypical ways, e.g., "hanging out" together, talking loudly, then a C.O. feels threatened, and quickly breaks them up. On the other hand, if Black prisoners do not conform to stereotypes, i.e., if they act individually, then they are often labelled as "putting on airs" or "having an attitude problem."[74] It is quite conceivable that such stereotypes would lead a C.O. to judge a Black as being a "security risk" and treat prisoner differently than White counterparts.

The interim report also indicates that racial segregation exists in most Ontario prisons as a result of a series of systemic practices. For example, over 80 per cent of prisoners transferred from Toronto prisons to the Hamilton-Wentworth Detention Centre are Black. This results in greater isolation of these prisoners as they are visited less by family and friends. This adds to their fear and anxiety about their forthcoming trials.

The authors of the interim report comment that "the separation between Black and White is striking"[75] referring to the segregated living areas in prisons. "Jamaican Blacks" are often segregated to their own areas in the Black section.

## Anti-Chinese Racism

The ideology which specifically targets people of Chinese origin for subjection to racism is referred to here as anti-Chinese racism, sometimes also referred to in sociological literature as sinophobia, orientalism and anti-orientalism. As discussed earlier, slave relations and other exploitative relations between Europeans and people of colour spawned various forms of racist ideologies.

In the 19th century, Europe was rapidly industrializing and thus had a vast need for raw materials. Africa, Asia, Latin America and the Caribbean became the scrambling grounds for European colonialists. Although China was not directly colonized or settled as in the case of India and the Caribbean, for example, it was indirectly controlled through exploitive trade by the British, French, Germans, Russians and Americans. As a result, Chinese people have been subjected to racist ideologies.

Ward[76] discusses that accounts by merchants, diplomats and missionaries after 1800 – the period of European penetration into China – depicted Chinese people as ignorant, perverse, cruel and poor. According to these ideologues, the glory of ancient China seems to have been replaced by "Chinese deceit, cunning, idolatry, despotism, xenophobia, cruelty, infanticide and intellectual and sexual perversity."[77] In other words, the "Orient", sometimes synonymous with "Asian", was depicted as the exact opposite of the "West" or "the European." This process of defining the "other", in this case, the Chinese and China, by Europeans resulted in "Orientalism", as conceptualized by Edward Said.[78] Said argues that Orientalism allows Europeans to "understand, in some cases, to control, manipulate, even incorporate, what is a manifestly different world."[79] Chan says that Orientalism reflected the "pattern of strength" between Asia and the West, with Asia being subordinated to the West.[80]

When Chinese immigrants entered Canada around 1858, during the Fraser River gold rush, North American popular culture already had a foundation in racism against Black and Native Peoples. Moreover, Orientalism was also a legacy, which surfaced from time to time in the form of anti-Chinese racism in various mining communities in North America. In British Columbia, the province of first entry into Canada, anti-Chinese racism seemed to flare up after 1866 during a period of economic recession.[81] The immigrants' experiences of systemic and institutionalized racism as workers, as men and women, and as community members within the Canadian political economy was rationalized by orientalist stereotypes and prejudices. For those in power, Orientalist ideas rationalized the process of "making cheap" Chinese labour which allowed them to proceed with nation building and with industrial development. Apart from mining and railway construction, Chinese workers were recruited in land clearing, public works, canning, lumbering, gardening and domestic work. Chinese workers earned one-half to one-third less than their White counterparts.[82] However, Chinese workers generally worked in areas where Whites did not want to work. It was only during times of unemployment that White workers competed for jobs usually done by Chinese-Canadians. For White workers, Orientalism provided them with a scapegoat in times of economic crisis and led them to further isolate Chinese workers from the labour movements of the time. Moreover, White workers by and large supported all exclusionist policies aimed at Chinese-Canadians.

Chinese-Canadians were disenfranchised in 1875 and subsequently from various provincial franchises, in Saskatchewan (1908), in Ontario (1914) and in British Columbia (1923). They were prohibited from working on government projects in 1876, from working underground in 1890, from public works in 1897, and from skilled jobs in coal mining in 1903. They could not hold liquor or hand-loggers' licenses. Such disenfranchisement meant exclusion from municipal offices, school boards, jury service, civil service, or professions in law and pharmacy.

After the Canadian Pacific Railway was completed, the Canadian government restricted Chinese immigration through a $50 head tax imposed on every Chinese person entering Canada in 1885. The head tax escalated to $100 in 1900 and to $500 in 1903. The 1923 Chinese Immigration Act finally stopped their immigration altogether apart from diplomatic corps, children born in Canada, merchants and students.

Some of the main characteristics of anti-Chinese sentiment in 19th century British Columbia have been described by Ward[83] as being alien, unassimilable, unclean, a threat to public health, morally depraved, erotically sensual, prone to opium addiction and to gambling, criminal, dishonest, and accustomed to low pay. Most Chinese women were seen as prostitutes and concubines. Overall, these descriptions amount to a prejudice among White British Columbians of the Chinese being "inferior." Ward[84] mentions that White employers used "industry, economy, sobriety, and law-abidingness" to characterized Chinese men when they needed cheap labourers to work for them; the sincerity behind such compliments is clearly questionable.

Chan[85] argues that the dominant image of early Chinese immigrants was that of being "sojourners", transients who held their loyalties to China and intended to be in Canada only temporarily to "make money". This image was projected in academic and popular texts and it became a stereotype of Chinese people. The sojourner image reinforced stereotypes of Chinese unassimilability, dishonesty and disloyalty.

However, it is clear that the exploitation of Chinese labourers and their subsequent systemic exclusion from various employment opportunities, political and civil rights actually compelled early Chinese immigrants to be alienated from the mainstream of Canadian life. They could not bring their spouses and children over to Canada because of immigration restrictions, neither could they develop a normal community life. The "temporary" status of Chinese male workers was not by choice but by imposition. By and large, working class women and children could not join their male relatives because of the head taxes. The few women who managed to come over were spouses of merchants and prostitutes. The latter were brought in small numbers to service the single, male Chinese workers.[86] Chan[87] argues that despite virulent anti-Asian sentiments and policies in Canada at that time, most Chinese-Canadians chose to remain in Canada.

Currently, Chinese-Canadians continue to be stigmatized, perhaps not as "sojourners", but as "immigrants", even when they are second or third generation Canadians. They continue to experience racism in the labour market. A 1991 survey[88] conducted among Chinese and non-Chinese social service providers in Canada showed that 63 per cent of the former and 59 per cent of the latter believed that Chinese-Canadians are discriminated against. In contrast, most manufacturing organizations, businesses and professional associations believed there was no discrimination against Chinese-Canadians.

Lack of communication skills is the most commonly cited[89] reason for employment difficulties of Chinese-Canadians, according to non-Chinese Canadians. This may indicate the prevalence of two of the most common stereotypes about Chinese-Canadians – that they do not speak English or that they are all "foreigners." Both these stereotypes are both linked to the sojourner image of the past. Second and third generation Chinese-Canadians tell of being put into English as Second Language (ESL) classes, or being asked if they can speak English.

Another popular modern stereotype about Chinese-Canadians is that they are "math and science whizzes". Emanating from this attitude is a fear that "they", the Asians, are taking over "Canadians", meaning Whites. The "Henry Fong" case in 1973 in Toronto highlighted these stereotypes and fears in the Medical School at the University of Toronto.[90] Henry Fong, a Chinese-Canadian medical student was expelled from Medical School within months of receiving his degree. The reasons were unclear and seemed to be based on orientalist notions about the Chinese, for example accusing him of dishonesty and referring to his "ethnic and cultural differences". This incident took place within an academic and medical establishment that was concerned about "foreign-born students", particularly "Asians" taking positions away from "Canadians" in medical school. Their spokespeople made no distinctions between Chinese who were Canadian citizens, immigrants or foreign students, thus implying that they were all "foreigners" and thus "non-Canadian."

In 1979, CTV's W5 program ran a show entitled "Campus Giveaway", which alleged that foreign students, mainly of Chinese origins, were taking away positions from Canadians.[91] Again, the journalists made no distinction between the immigration and citizenship status of Chinese-Canadians in medical school. Thus, they were all depicted as foreigners. Further research[92] by members of the Chinese-Canadian community revealed that there were in fact only two students on student visas out of 256 students in the first year of medical school at the University of Toronto, which W5 had used as a prime example. After a year of protests and various forms of social action coordinated by the Ad Hoc Committee of the Council of Chinese Canadians in Ontario Against W5, CTV made a full public apology to Chinese-Canadians.

Another current stereotype about Chinese-Canadians is that they are all rich.[93] This myth, which is class and gender-based, originated because most of the people who came under Canada's immigrant investor program since 1986 have been from Hong Kong and Taiwan. This program allows Canadian landed status to immigrants with $500,000 or more to invest in Canada. Still, Wong[94] points out that only five per cent of immigrants from Hong Kong and Taiwan have come under this program.

In contrast to this myth, the reality is that Chinese-Canadian males earn 30 per cent less than Canadian males overall and Chinese-Canadian females earn 40 per cent less than Canadian females.[95] It is true that Chinese-Canadians are over-represented in professional fields in terms of their proportion in the overall population, but they are actually under-represented relative to their qualification and skills. Many of these professionals are underemployed in marginal positions.[96]

A 1977 survey conducted in the Grange Community in South-East Spadina, a concentration of Chinese residence in Toronto, revealed that 35 per cent were unskilled and semi-skilled. In another area in Broadview, Toronto, 40 per cent were unskilled and semi-skilled. There is a big concentration of Chinese-Canadian workers in the service sector – in restaurants, hotels, and garment industries. It is estimated that there are 3,000 Chinese-Canadians working in the Toronto garment industry, most of them women.

A survey[97] conducted among Indo-Chinese refugees in Toronto revealed that none of them were working in professional, managerial and commercial positions. Most of them were in "blue-collar" work in textile and metal industries and others were janitors, kitchen helpers, waitresses, busboys and maids. Indo-Chinese refugees were more likely to be in blue-collar work compared to other immigrant groups and Canadian-born. They were poorly paid, underemployed and experienced downward mobility. Women were more disadvantaged than men.

When it comes to Chinese-Canadian women, there are particular stereotypes which reflect racism and sexism combined. Tajima[98] describes two basic types of stereotypes portrayed in the commercial media, namely the "Lotus Blossom Baby", and the "Dragon Lady". The former encompasses the images of the China doll, geisha girl and shy Polynesian beauty. The latter includes prostitutes and "devious madames". It is interesting to reflect on the Lotus Blossom Baby image in the context of the experiences of a significant number of Chinese-Canadian women who work in subordinate positions in the garment industry.

Tajima and others[99] elaborate on this stereotype as depicting Chinese women as passive, compliant, and servile to men. They are seen as soft, romantic objects for White men, ultra-feminine, delicate, and welcome alternatives to White, "liberated" women, (a stereotype in itself). Love relationships between Asian women and White European men are often portrayed as being socially unacceptable and the children of such unions as unfortunate orphans. The fear of inter-racial marriages and miscegenation is resolved in the media by the suicide, illness or death of these sacrificing mothers. This particular collection of stereotypes was greatly reinforced by two decades of neo-colonial rule in Vietnam by the U.S., including military aggression, where unequal and oppressive relations between the U.S. and Vietnam in general and racist patriarchal relationships between Vietnamese women and U.S. soldiers were the norm.

In Elson's[100] discussion of workplace ideologies, we find the translation of popular stereotypes about Chinese, Japanese and other Asian women onto the paid work circuit. The following is an advertisement in a Malaysian brochure aimed at attracting multinational companies:

> The manual dexterity of the Oriental female is famous the world over. Her hands are small and she works fast with extreme care. Who, therefore could be better qualified by nature and inheritance to contribute to the efficiency of a production line than the Oriental girl?[101]

She has been objectified and depicted as a machine as if her hands are automatic and severed from the rest of her being. The myth of the "submissive, Oriental girl" makes them very attractive to western capitalists in search of "cheap" and "efficient" labour. A biological explanation is offered to explain the apparent passivity and nimbleness of Asian women. The daily struggles of such women workers are ignored by these orientalists and also the role of militaristic governments in crushing any form of worker resistance in many Asian countries is not mentioned. The "nimbleness" which is learned by many women at home due to gender socialization is taken as a genetic given for which she is not valued or paid.

Stam[102] explores the various ways in which racist and colonialist ideas and images are reproduced by the media, particularly by cinema and television. According to Stam, "colonial-style racism" includes some of the following elements: portraying the stigmatized as being deficient, blaming the victim, devaluing the lives of the stigmatized, sometimes advocating their genocide, the denial of difference and at the same time the denial of sameness. These are transmitted not only through plot and characterization but also through such cinematic elements as lighting, framing and music.

Rosemary Brown[103] has discussed that by the age of two and a half, children begin to develop racial awareness; a realization that people "look " different. This is followed by a phase in which children develop racial identity, i.e., a sense of belonging in a "race" and then a third phase, racial preference, where they develop an awareness of white supremacy in the larger society and therefore desire to be a part of the "preferred race." By the age of seven or eight, children can become full-blown racists depending on various environmental factors, for instance the level of racial tension in society. Education, media and popular culture are all key socializing agents in terms of racializing, gendering and classing individuals.

## Notes

1. The addition of "everynight" realities as an integral part of our lives is borrowed from Dorothy Smith, "Feminist Reflections on Political Economy," in *Feminism in Action: Studies in Political Economy* (Toronto: Canadian Scholars' Press, 1992), p.1-21.
2. Karl Marx, "Preface To A Contribution To The Karl Marx Critique of Political Economy" in Erich Fromm, *Marx's Concept of Man* (New York: Frederick Unger Pub., 1981).
3. Michael Burawoy, "Towards a Marxist Theory of the Labour Process. Braverman and Beyond," *Politics and Society*, 8, 3-4(1978).
4. James W. Rinehart, *The Tyranny of Work* (Canada: Longman Canada Ltd., 1975); Seymour Faber, "Working Class Organization," *Our Generation*, II, 2(1975).
5. Richard Edwards, *Contested Terrain* (New York: Basic Books Inc., 1979).
6. Andrew Herman, "Conceptualizing Control: Domination and Hegemony in the Capitalist Labour Process," *The Insurgent Sociologist*, Vol. 11, No. 3 (Fall, 1982).
7. Lastly Papp and Royson James, "Blacks Still Shut Out Of Boardrooms Despite Promise of More Opportunity," *Toronto Star*, January 16, 1989, p.A1.
8. Frances Henry and Effie Ginzberg, *No Discrimination Here? Toronto Employers and the Multiracial Workforce. (Toronto*: Social Planning Council and Urban Alliance on Race Relations, 1985).
9. Urban Alliance on Race Relations, *The Second Annual Employment Equity Forum of the Urban Alliance on Race Relations, Verbatim Proceedings* (Toronto: Urban Alliance on Race Relations, 1990).
10. John Porter, *The Vertical Mosaic* (Toronto: The University of Toronto Press, 1965); Peter C. Pineo, "The Social Standing of Ethnic and Racial Groupings" in Jay E. Goldstein and Rita M. Bienvenue (eds) *Ethnic Relations in Canada* (Toronto: Butterworths, 1985); Marlene Mackie, "Ethnic Stereotype and Prejudice: Alberta Indians, Hutterites and Ukrainians" in Goldstein and Bienvenue (eds) *Ethnic Relations in Canada*, 1985.
11. Tracey Tyler, "Burning Issue," *Toronto Star*, January 31, 1993, p. B1-B8.

12. Papp and James, "Blacks Still Shut Out."

13. Harish Jain, "Draft Employment Equity Bill Needs Major Overhaul," *Toronto Star*, August 28, 1993, p. A23.

14. Quoted in Nandita Sharma, "Restructuring Society, Restructuring Lives: The Global Restructuring of Capital and Women's Paid Employment in Canada," *Socialist Studies Bulletin*, No. 37 (July-September, 1994) p. 27.

15. Ibid.

16. Discussed in Harvey J. Krahn and Graham S. Lowe, *Work, Industry and Canadian Society* (Canada: Nelson Canada, 1988), p.84.

17. David M. Gordon, Richard Edwards, Michael Reich, *Segmented Work, Divided Workers* (Cambridge: Cambridge University Press, 1982).

18. Charlene Gannage, *Double Day, Double Bind* (Toronto: The Women's Press, 1986), p.14.

19. Gordon et al, *Segmented Work*.

20. Jeffrey G. Reitz, *Ethnicity and Inequality and Segregation in Jobs* (Toronto: University of Toronto, 1981).

21. Frances Henry and Carol Tator, "Fleming's Racism Poll Raises Old Questions With Few Answers," *Toronto Star*, March 31, 1982.

22. Frances Henry and Effie Ginzberg, *Who Gets the Work? A Test of Racial Discrimination in Employment* (Toronto: Social Planning Council and Urban Alliance on Race Relations, 1985).

23. Rosalie Abella, *Equality in Employment*, A Commission Report, Ottawa, November, 1984.

24. Papp and James, "Blacks Still Shut Out."

25. Quoted in Sharma, "Restructuring Society," p. 22.

26. Ibid, p.21.

27. Wilson Head, *An Exploratory Study of Attitudes and Perceptions of Minority and Majority Group Healthcare Workers* (Ontario: Ministry of Labour, 1985).

28. Cynthia Cockburn, *Brothers* (London: Pluto Press, 1983); Ann Game and Rosemary Pringle, *Gender At Work* (Sydney: George Allen, 1983); Cynthia Cockburn, *Machinery of Dominance: Women, Men and Technical Knowledge* (London: Pluto Press, 1985).

29. Tania Das Gupta, *Degradation and Deskilling: the Case of the Garment Industry in Toronto*. Ph.D. thesis, University of Toronto, 1986; Edwards, *Contested Terrain*; Gordon et al, *Segmented Work*.

30. Quoted in Henry and Ginzberg, *Who Gets the Work*, p. 11.

31. Angus Reid Group, *Highlights of Attitudes about Multiculturalism and Citizenship* (Canada: Multiculturalism and Citizenship, 1991).

32. Frances Henry and Effie Ginzberg, *No Discrimination Here? Toronto Employers and the Multiracial Workforce* (Toronto: Social Planning Council and Urban Alliance on Race Relations, 1985b).

33. Allan Andrew, "Auditing Race Relations Practices of Metro Police," *Currents*, Vol. 8, No. 1 (June, 1993), p. 14-16.

34. Final Report and Summary of Information Gathered From Service Providers,

Residents and Racial Minority Community Organizations in the Jane-Finch Community Regarding the Quality of Police-Minority Community Relations," Unpublished Paper, Toronto, January 6, 1989.

35. Ontario Women's Directorate, *Workplace Harassment: An Action Guide for Women* (Ontario: Ontario Women's Directorate, 1994), p.2.

36. Canadian Civil Liberties Association, Letter from A. Alan Borovoy to The Honourable Bob Mackenzie, Toronto, January 18, 1991.

37. Jane Allan, *Employment Equity: How We Can Use It To Fight Workplace Racism* (Toronto: Cross Cultural Communication Centre, 1988).

38. Henry and Ginzberg, *Who Gets the Work?*

39. Ontario Human Rights Commission, *The Experience of Visible Minorities in the Work World: the Case of MBA Graduates* (Ontario: OHRC, 1983).

40. Ontario Women's Directorate, *Workplace Harassment: An Action Guide for Women* (Ontario: Ontario Women's Directorate, 1994), p.6.

41. Charlotte Morgan, "Speaking Out On Racism: An Interview with Enid Lee," *OPSTF News*, April 1989, p.6-9; Allan, *Employment Equity*.

42. Peggy McIntosh, "White Privilege: Unpacking the Invisible Knapsack," *Peace and Freedom*, (July-August, 1989).

43. William K. Tabb, "Capitalism, Colonization and Racism," *The Review of Radical Political Economics*, Vol. 3, No. 3 (Summer, 1971); Oliver Cox, *Caste, Class and Race* (New York: Doubleday & Co. Inc., 1948).

44. Papp and James, "Blacks Shut Out."

45. Corinne Sparks, *Women of Colour in the Legal Profession: A Panoply of Multiple Discrimination*, Appendix 10 to the Report of the Canadian Bar Association Task Force on Gender Equality in the Legal Profession, Halifax, Nova Scotia, August, 1993.

46. Henry and Ginzberg, *Who Gets the Work*, p.59.

47. Bobby Si, "The Bubble Bursts: the Coming Crises of the Chinese Community," *Assignation*, Vol. 4, No.2 (July, 1982), p.2-6.

48. Reitz, *Ethnicity and Inequality*.

49. Institute of Race Relations, *Patterns of Racism, Book 2* (England: Institute of Race Relations, 1982).

50. Terry Wotherspoon, (ed.), "Introduction: Conflict and Crisis in Canadian Education" in *The Political Economy of Education* (Toronto: Methuen Publications, 1987), p. 7.

51. bell hooks, *Black Looks: Race and Representation* (Toronto: Between the Lines, 1992).

52. Angela Davis, *Women, Race and Class* (London: The Women's Press, 1981).

53. Dionne Brand, "Black Women and Work: The Impact of Racially Constructed Gender Roles on the Sexual Division of Labour: Part 1," *Fireweed*, Issue 25 (Fall, 1987), p. 28-37.

54. Esmeralda Thornhill, "Focus on Black Women" in *Race, Class, Gender: Bonds and Barriers* edited by Vorst, Das Gupta et al (Canada: Society for Socialist Studies, 1991).

55. Thornhill, "Focus", p. 33.

56. Davis, *Women, Race*.

57. Thornhill, "Focus."

58. Davis, *Women, Race*, p.23.

59. hooks, *Black Looks*, p.54.

60. bell hooks, *Ain't I A Woman: Black Women and Feminism* (Boston: South End Press, 1981).

61. Garnet McDiarmid and David Pratt, *Teaching Prejudice* (Toronto: Ontario Institute of Studies in Education, 1967).

62. hooks, *Black Looks*.

63. James W. St. G. Walker, *Racial Discrimination in Canada: The Black Experience* (Canada: Canadian Historical Association, 1985).

64. John Spears, "Africville Won't Die, Blacks Vow," *Toronto Star*, July 29, 1991, p.A14.

65. Maureen Murray, "Blacks Call For Action After Riot in Halifax," *Toronto Star*, July, 1991, p.A1.

66. Nova Scotia Advisory Group on Race Relations, *Report of the Nova Scotia Advisory Group on Race Relations*, Nova Scotia, 1991.

67. Nova Scotia Advisory Group, *Report*, p.3.

68. Andrew Duffy, "Blacks Near Ghettos, Study Says," *Toronto Star*, October 7, 1991, p. A1-A7.

69. Stephen Lewis, *The Stephen Lewis Report*, Toronto, June 9, 1992.

70. Court of Appeal for Ontario, *Between Her Majesty the Queen and Carlton Parks*, October 20, 1992.

71. Court of Appeal, *Between Her Majesty*, p. 29.

72. Commission on Systemic Racism on the Ontario Criminal Justice System, *Racism Behind Bars: The Treatment of Black and Other Racial Minority Prisoners in Ontario Prisons*. (Ontario: Queen's Printer for Ontario, 1994).

73. Ibid, p.23.

74. Ibid, p.21.

75. Ibid, p.57.

76. W. Peter Ward, *White Canada Forever* (Montreal: McGill Queen's University Press, 1978).

77. Ward, *White Canada*, p.4.

78. Edward W. Said, *Orientalism* (London: Routledge & Kegan Paul, 1978).

79. Quoted in Stuart Scharr, "Orientalism At the Service of Imperialism," *Race and Class*, Vol. XXI, No. 1 (Summer, 1979), p.67-79.

80. Anthony B. Chan, "Orientalism and Image Making: the Sojourner in Canadian History," *The Journal of Ethnic Studies*, Vol. 9, No. 3 (Fall, 1981), p.37-46.

81. Peter S. Li, *The Chinese in Canada* (Toronto: Oxford University Press, 1988).

82. Ward, *White Canada*, p. 17.

83. Ward, *White Canada*, p.4-35.

84. Ward, ibid, p.11.

85. Chan, "Orientalism."

86. Discussed in Tania Das Gupta, "Families of Native Peoples, Immigrants and, People of Colour," in Nancy Mandell and Ann Duffy (eds.) *Canadian Families: Diversity, Conflict and Change* (Canada: Harcourt Brace, 1995), p.141-174.

87. Chan, ibid.

88. Virginia Galt, "Chinese Canadians Fight Racism," *Globe and Mail*, April 26, 1991, p. A7.

89. Ibid.

90. "Come To Henry Fong's Appeal," unpublished document, Chinese Canadian National Council, Toronto, 1973.

91. Cheuk Kwan, "The Anti-W5 Movement," *Combatting Racism in the Workplace Readings Kit* (Toronto: Cross Cultural Communication Centre, 1983.

92. Cheuk Kwan, "The Foreign Threat That Never Was," *The Asianadian*, Vol. 2, No. 3 (Winter, 1979-80), p.21-22.

93. Joseph Wong, "Some Myths About Hong Kong Immigrants," *Toronto Star*, October 15, 1992; Winnie Ng, Roger Kwan, Mr. Law, Wai Man Lee, "A Chinese Workers' Perspective on Canadian Society," in *Effective Citizenship in Canada's Multicultural Society –a Chinese Perspective*, Proceedings of the Inter-cultural Conference, Council of Chinese Canadians in Ontario, Toronto, April 8-9, 1978.

94. Ibid.

95. Chinese Canadian National Council, *Brief to the Honourable Gregory Sorbara, Minister Responsible for Women's Issues*, March 29, 1988.

96. Bobby Siu, "The Employment of Indo-Chinese Refugees in Toronto," Paper Presented at Conference of Council of Chinese Canadians in Ontario, Toronto, November 10-11, 1979.

97. Ibid.

98. Renee E. Tajima, "Lotus Blossoms Don't Bleed: Images of Asian Women," in *Making Waves: An Anthology of Writings By and About Asian American Women* edited by Asian Women United of California. (Boston: Beacon Press, 1989).

99. U.S Commission on Civil Rights, "Commerical T.V. – the Portrayal of Women and Minorities," *Window Dressing on the Set: Women and Minorities on T.V.*, August, 1977, p.5-8.

100. Diane Elson, "Nimble Fingers and Other Fables," in Wendy Chapkis and Cynthia Enloe (eds.), *Of Common Cloth: Women in the Global Textile Industry* (Amsterdam: Transnational Institute, 1983).

101. Ibid, p.6.

102. Robert Stam, "From Stereotype to Discourse: Methodological Reflexions on Racism in the Media," *Cineaction*, No. 32 (Fall, 1993), p. 10-29.

103. Rosemary Brown, "Children and Racism," *Multiculturalism*, Vol.III, No.2 (1979), p. 19-22.

**Chapter 2**

# Manifestations of Racism from Management

THIS CHAPTER provides examples of how management practices can create an environment for systemic racism.

The following manifestations, described in a) to d) relate to management's perception of what constitutes a "threat" from workers of colour and management's efforts to preserve their own power. The perceived threat from workers of colour may be related to the everyday culture of racism.

### a) Targeting

Targeting occurs when one worker is singled out for differential treatment – harsher scrutiny, severe discipline or less desirable work assignments. Targeting is usually used to isolate, silence and fire a worker of colour. Workers of colour may be subjected to racial name-calling by co-workers, threatened physically or fired arbitrarily. It is not unusual for racist assailants to be untouched by management. Therefore, the victim of racism is actually being blamed and punished by the targeting process.

Workers of colour are often targeted when they demand their rights as workers. The challenge to management is an ultimate show of power in the workplace and those who dare demonstrate it are usually silenced and "taught a lesson". The bottom line is that management does not like workers who do not toe *their* line because it threatens power relations in the workplace. The targeting of grievers and union activists has been confirmed by the Ontario Coalition of Black Trade Unionists.[1] It seems that for workers of colour there is a differential level of tolerance of challenge as far as White management is concerned. What would be seen as "constructive criticism" in White workers is seen as "insubordination" in workers of colour.

### b) Scapegoating

Scapegoating of workers is a common management practice in many workplaces. One worker of colour, or a group of workers of colour, will be blamed for something, while White workers will not. The "criminality" of people of colour is a common racial stereotype. This accusation can be later used to deny workers of colour privileges or rights given to White workers.

### c) Excessive Monitoring

Another form of harassment is excessive monitoring and documentation to be used against a worker of colour. This practice also implies that workers of colour need more guidance, more corrections, and less independence given the inferiority of their labour power. These are based on stereotypes from slavery and colonialism. Increased monitoring can lead to increased discipline by management, with has a negative effect on promotional chances.

### d) Marginalization

Management may marginalize or isolate a worker of colour and thereby diminish her sense of security in the workplace. Workers of colour are excluded from cliques and "old boy's networks", which affect their promotional chances.

The manifestations described as e) to j) in the following section relate to largely unconscious stereotypical assumptions, which influence the way workers of colour are perceived by White management. These stereotypical assumptions are reflected in management actions which adversely impact on workers of colour.

### e) Seeing Solidarity As A Threat

Management may see friendship and solidarity among workers of colour as threatening managerial authority. This is ironic, as racial segregation, i.e., the clumping of workers of colour into similar jobs, is also a way in which management sometimes controls workers. The perceived threat from the solidarity of Black workers for instance may be a reflection of common notions of Black people being "crazy", "evil" and "treacherous", stereotypes emanating from Black resistance to slavery.

Management may deal with the perceived threat of workers of colour by dispersing or separating these workers, or by strongly discouraging their association. Such management practices can be seen as an extreme reaction to class or racial opposition.

### f) Infantalization

Condescension, belittlement, or implying that a worker of colour is "not good enough", are all subtle ways in which a person can be harassed. In the process, the person's dignity, self-worth and adulthood are reduced. Henry and Ginzberg[2] document White managers saying that workers of colour are "lowering standards" or are "incompetent". These are extensions of negative evaluations of the labour of people of colour and their supposed child-like, "close to nature" status, ideologies emanating from colonialism and slavery.

### g) Blaming the Victim

Management will often blame workers of colour for their own misfortunes, including their experience of racism. Young[3] writes that complainants to the Ontario Human Rights Commission (OHRC) are often viewed as "excitable", "lacking in credibility", "oversensitive" or "lacking in objectivity". The implications are that charges of racism by workers of colour are frequently seen as untrue, exaggerated or a figment of their imagination. Hence, with this practice of blaming the victim, racism is denied and the status quo is maintained. Moreover, workers who confront racist management practices are often branded as "troublemakers" and "unable to get along with others,"[4] and their resulting alienation from their co-workers is often used by management to discipline or dismiss them. Assumptions about their inherent dishonesty, unreliability and "chip-on-the-shoulder" attitudes underlie these management practices. These assumptions are part of racial prejudice, learned over generations by White people.

### h) Bias in Work Allocation

Differential workloads on the basis of racist stereotypes is a common management practice, perpetuated systemically through hiring and promotional systems. In almost every case where racism in the workplace has been pointed out, it has been shown that Black workers and other workers of colour have been assigned the heaviest, dirtiest, poorly paid, and least secure jobs in relation to the work assigned to White workers. Moreover, stereotyping different ethnic groups often results in a division of labour in the workplace which further isolates and divides them. Black women, for instance, are affected by racialized, sexist stereotypes emanating from the history of slavery in the Americas. They are expected to perform physically demanding jobs in a way which defies standards of White, European femininity. They are also seen as nurturing in an intuitive manner, while being open to performing work which non-Blacks consider unacceptable. Thus, it is common to find an over-representation of Black women in domestic work, eldercare and lower levels of nursing. They may not be as well represented in sales, waitressing, receptionist and middle-managerial positions. White women of European origin are seen as being more suitable to such jobs.

### i) Underemployment and the Denial of Promotions

Underemployment and the denial of promotion frequently go hand in hand. A worker of colour may be subjected to differential treatment and denied access to new job openings. She may also be refused training or upgrading by her supervisor and then blamed for "incompetence". At the same time, she may find that her White counterparts with less qualifications and experience are being mentored and eventually promoted. Such differential promotional practices perpetuate deep rooted racial stereotypes against workers of colour, such as their inherent inferiority and their intrinsic knack for doing physical as opposed to mental labour.

### j) Lack of Accommodation

Accommodation may be obstructed or denied to workers of colour because a White manager suspects workers are being dishonest about their illness or disability. Suspicion may be expressed in a variety of ways, from minimizing their complaints, inflexibility regarding health policies, to punishing rather than accommodating the complainant. Prejudging, assuming that people of colour are dishonest and lazy, is at the root of such management reactions.

The following sections, k) to m), identify management practices which divide workers and play them off against each other. In the end, this adversely affects workers of colour because it reduces their solidarity and bargaining power.

### k) Segregation of Workers

Management hires men and women workers of diverse ethnic/racial backgrounds and then employs them separately in homogenous segments. This results in shifts, task groups, and work areas defined by ethnicity, race or gender. In 1982, a well-publicized human rights case involved a factory in Ontario[5] where the night shift was entirely composed of South Asian women, while the day shift was predominantly White. This enabled management to practice differential policies for different groups of workers and also to play the games of divide and rule. The night shift was denied a pay increase of 30 cents an hour, which had already been granted to the day shift.

In this case, racial and ethnic segmentation enabled management to super-exploit workers of colour as "cheap" labour. It also kept them separated from workers who were White and from other cultural backgrounds, so that they could not compare notes or show an united front. Brand and Bhaggiyadatta[6] write of an union organizer in a garment shop who tells about the failure of a union drive because of the antagonism of two groups of workers in the factory, namely the Greek and Chinese workers. Management played on the differences between the two groups by giving them piecework, and paying them differential prices per piece. Chinese workers, lacked seniority, worked the night shift, and gave in to management tactics. They voted against the union.

### l) Co-optation and Selective Alliances

Allying oneself with management against co-workers may be a pragmatic strategy in the face of racism, recession and the lack of employment alternatives. The person who is co-opted to participate in targeting a worker of colour may be a token supervisor of colour, a White worker or a worker of colour. In the first scenario, the supervisor may be motivated by fear or may be a victim of harassment. In the second scenario, the White worker may have volunteered to harass a worker of colour in the hopes of being in management's "good books". In the third scenario, a worker of colour may volunteer to "spy" on her colleagues of colour in the hopes of getting ahead in her career, similar to the White worker in the second scenario.

All of these management allies may remain silent in the face of oppression and refuse to challenge management because of the fear of losing their job. Or, they may genuinely feel they are doing a "good deed" for the company.

### m) Tokenism

It is common practice for management to deny racism in the workplace by hiring one or two workers of colour in positions of authority, and then citing that as an excuse for not addressing the problem. The lack of an ethnically or racially balanced representation among management leaves the organization open to biased employment systems, which in turn results in a variety of racist manifestations, some of which I have mentioned.

The next chapter closely examines the garment industry and analyzes race and gender relations as they operate on systemic, everyday and attitudinal bases, identifying the management practices discussed in this chapter.

### Notes

1. OCBTU, 1987-88, p.9.
2. Henry and Ginzberg, *No Discrimination Here?*
3. Donna Young, *The Donna Young Report: The Handling of Race Discrimination Complaints At the Ontario Human Rights Commission*, Toronto, October 23, 1992.
4. Ibid., p. 24.
5. Leslie Scrivener, "Fight For Promised Raise Leaves 23 Women Jobless," *Toronto Star*, Nov. 23, 1982, p. D18.
6. Dionne Brand and Krisantha Sri Bhaggiyadatta, *Rivers Have Sources, Trees Have Roots: Speaking of Racism* (Toronto: Cross Cultural Communication Centre, 1986), p.141.

## Chapter 3

# Racism in the
# Garment Industry

### Introduction and Research Methods

Toronto's garment industry within national and international development is the focus of this chapter. My research in this industry has involved a number of techniques over the past 13 years. I have read historical reports, union documents and secondary literature on this industry and then supplemented that with in-depth personal interviews with garment workers. The latter were conducted in two time periods. The first group of interviews was held between 1981 and 1985 with garment workers contacted through the Toronto office of the International Ladies Garment Workers Union (ILGWU) and through various personal contacts within the South Asian and Greek communities.[1] The second group of interviews is currently in progress. These involve homeworkers, particularly within the South Asian and Spanish-speaking communities in Toronto.

### The Big Picture: Political Economy of the Industry

The garment industry is marked by its vulnerability to low-wage import competition, its low capacity for technological innovation and its historical dependence on the cheapened labour of immigrant women and women of colour.

Although garment factories, are both large and small, they mainly fall into the smaller, highly competitive sector. The industry is fragile, with workshops having less than 50 workers. Even in established shops, the total workforce varies depending on seasonal fluctuations as well as product demand. The industry is one of the six most vulnerable to imports.

Given this vulnerability, garment manufacturers have remained competitive by minimizing production cost through labour-intensive production processes. Production costs have been minimized by utilizing "cheaper" forms of labour, primarily that of women and people of colour in Canada and also by relocating to countries in the Third World where low wages predominate and repression of labour organizations is state policy.

Another way of remaining competitive within Canada has been to establish protectionist policies in an effort to restrict import penetration. If we look at government policies towards the textile and garment industries in the post-war period, we find that the strategy has been of "managed trade over competition, of protection over adjustment."[2] This strategy was institutionalized in 1970 in a Canadian Textile Policy. In 1974, protectionism involved selective and voluntary import restraints steered by the international Multi-Fibre Agreement (MFA). In 1976, protectionism became more pronounced when temporary global import restrictions were imposed to respond to severe crises in the textile and garment industries. MFAs were renewed in 1977, 1981, 1986, 1991 and 1993. However, larger, multinational companies could avoid limitations set by the MFA by getting their garments shipped from different source countries. On one hand, protectionist import policies have been aimed mainly at low-cost sources, principally in Asia. On the other hand, there has been a tendency to liberalize trade with the U.S. since the early 1970s by means of duty drawbacks and tariff concessions.[3] Larger companies adjusted themselves to a free trade environment. In 1988, imports had risen at an annual rate of 7.1 per cent, while exports grew at a rate of 4.8 per cent.[4] In 1989, the Canadian government signed a free-trade agreement with the U.S. and the North American Free Trade Agreement (NAFTA) in 1994, brought Mexico into the fold. This has provided the avenue for larger garment manufacturers to shut their Canadian plants and open new plants in lower-wage areas in the Southern U.S. and Mexico. As far as the MFA is concerned, it was decided in 1993 that the agreement would be phased out over a 10-year period.[5] Smaller manufacturers have simply gone bankrupt or closed factories, and are employing homeworkers. The world is a playing field for the multinational garment companies.

Efforts to restructure and rationalize the industry, and to "adjust" workers displaced by these processes were undertaken by the Textile and Clothing Board (TCB) established in 1970 and by the Canadian Industrial Renewal Board (CIRB) set up in 1981. However, these strategies did not affect most garment factories, as they are small and have less access to investment capital. Even in larger factories, only designing, pattern making and cutting were computerized, but sewing remained labour intensive. The TCB and the CIRB were replaced by the Canadian International Trade Tribunal in 1988.

Employment in the garment industry in Canada fell from 95,800 in 1988 to 62,300 in 1992.[6] In Ontario, employment fell from 27,700 in 1988 to 16,800 in 1993. At present, the industry in Canada is re-organizing fundamentally; "homework" has become the crucial link, keeping smaller manufacturers (contractors) afloat and keeping multinational garment enterprises competitive, as many of them employ the contractors to "get their production done." Homeworkers are those who manufacture or assemble commodities or provide services from home to an employer who frequently acts as a contractor for a large company. Homeworkers are usually paid piece wages, and studies have revealed that most of them are super-exploited, being paid less than minimum wages and grossly over-worked. Homeworkers do not own capital, they do not control their own labour process and they do not employ others, although they may be assisted by unpaid family members.

A description of the various stages of garment production may be useful in understanding the nature of the re-organization process. The making of a garment begins with a designer making a sample of a garment, followed by a cardboard replica being created in a standard size. Next, a cutter makes a number of samples of the garment in different sizes. This process is called grading. The samples in different sizes are then marked out on a big sheet of paper based on the number of garments and the sizes specified by a supervisor. This is called marker-making. Grading and marker-making are now computerized in many shops. Next, layers of cloth are laid out under the marker and then a cutter cuts along the marker edges. The pieces are then bundled by bundlers according to size and colour. The pieces are then sewn by sewing machine operators with underpressers pressing seams in between. Finishers trim, fit buttons, clean and prepare garments for the final pressing. The garments are pressed by top pressers and finally packed and shipped to buyers.[7]

Lipsig-Mumme[8] has described what can happen to work organization in garment shops when they re-organize due to import competition and the capitalist need to take advantage of free continental trade opportunities. She has cited this process as it has taken place in Montreal, historically the centre of the garment industry in Canada. She has characterized this process as a "gender specific tactic" of economic restructuring. I would argue that it could also be considered as being "ethno-race specific" given that many of the affected workers are immigrant women. Lipsig-Mumme presents case studies of two garment shops in Montreal which restructured in the mid-1980s. A large shop with 350 workers simply relocated its sewing and finishing to Asia, while retaining a "newly-opened non-union cutting shop." A medium-sized shop with 50 workers could not afford to relocate its enterprise elsewhere, and in order to remain competitive it re-opened a non-union cutting shop and engaged the services of a contractor, who in turn hired homeworkers to sew and do finishing jobs. Lipsig-Mumme also points out that 80 to 90 per cent of workers who lost their factory jobs were women. Although she did not report their ethnicity, race or immigrant status, it would be realistic to surmise that many of these women were immigrants.

An important factor pointed out by Lipsig-Mumme is the de-unionization that accompanies this re-organization process. In Ontario, a similar pattern is also evident. Since 1988, 42 unionized factories have closed.[9] De-unionization implies disempowerment and lack of bargaining strength in a labour market where employers control wages and the nature of the labour process. The "cheapness" of the labour of these women and people of colour are predicated on this disempowerment. Lipsig-Mumme estimates that in 1981, about 20,000 homeworkers were sewing in Montreal.

The rise of homeworkers in British Columbia has been pointed out by Ocran, Hyndman and Jamieson[10] who write that there are an estimated 3,000 homeworkers in that province, most of whom are in garment manufacturing. The rise of these homeworkers has been connected to economic restructuring of which globalization is an intrinsic part. Ocran et al also point out that in the garment industry there seems to be a two-tier system where more expensive garments are produced by "specialized" workers who work in shops, retain more control over their labour process and employ more sophisticated machinery while the inexpensive, basic and "high turn-over" styles tend to be produced by homeworkers.

In Toronto, an ILGWU study[11] revealed that there had been a tremendous growth in contract shops in Ontario in the preceding 20 years. In 1971, only four contract shops had been registered, whereas over 116 shops were registered in 1991. These shops presumably employ few factory workers and a large number of homeworkers. The ILGWU in Toronto estimates there are between 2,000 to 4,000 homeworkers in the metropolitan area. In a 1993 brief presented to the Government of Ontario Special Committee on NAFTA, the ILGWU (Ontario District) presented a case study of Vogue Bra that operated a large shop in Cambridge, Ontario, employing 80 workers. By 1992, the plant closed after it had downsized to 40 workers. The ILGWU discovered that soon after closing its Cambridge shop, the company opened a plant in a free trade zone (maquiladora) in Mexico, where workers are paid as little as 50 cents an hour. One also wonders if some of Vogue's Canadian production was being contracted out to homeworkers and to subcontractors.

By 1993, the ILGWU[12] in Toronto had developed an even clearer picture of the reorganized chain of production in the industry. The industry is controlled by multinational retailers, e.g., The Hudson Bay Company, Eaton's and Dylex, who control as much as 40 per cent of the Canadian market.[13] There are also large manufacturers who may design garments, determine when they are needed and how much to pay contractors. Small contract shops design, if that is not done by retailers, then cut the materials according to those designs. Finally, homeworkers sew the complete garments together. Here, we see a three-tiered system where a few large retailers are controlling the industry at the top, with a good number of contractors acting as intermediaries or middlepersons and an even larger number of homeworkers working at the bottom. This is a global system. It is reported that companies like The Bay also contract out garment manufacturing to suppliers in Indonesia, Thailand and the Philippines, where workers are forced to work at "slave" wages.[14] Retailers therefore save on inventory, storage space and supervisory costs. They also receive their supplies "just in time" facilitated by sophisticated computer technology. This type of enterprise has been termed a "hollow corporation".[15] The decentralizing of the actual production and supply of finished garments also facilitates circumventing the Multi-Fibre Arrangement (MFA) which has set up import and export quotas for various countries. The search for cheap and ever-ready labour seems to have no limit and one of the results of that is the dipping of wages all over the world, including

Canada, through the resurgence of homework. The advantage of retaining production in Canada for retailers and large manufacturers, predominantly North American and European, is the potential of maximizing "just-in-time" supplies. However, this provides an additional incentive for them to resort to contractors who employ homeworkers in order to minimize production costs and thereby remain competitive in the consumer market.

The rise of homework has obviously reduced the bargaining power of garment workers who work in factories and whose wages have historically[16] been very low. There has always been a wide variety of wages earned depending on union status, gender, ethnicity and race and these are often arbitrary. The piece-wage system is a dominant characteristic of this industry and homework or the "sweating system" is not a new feature. It has been prevalent since the inception of the industry in Canada around the 1870s.

The wages have been arbitrarily kept at rock bottom levels chiefly because piece workers have historically been non-English or French speaking, immigrant women and, more recently, women of colour. Child labour was prevalent well into the beginning of this century despite school laws for eight to 14 year olds. Even though child labour is illegal today, school-age children often help their mothers in such things as "turning belts, trimming seams, [and] packing bundles."[17] More modern reports have confirmed the continuity of low wages and deplorable working conditions in this industry. While posing as a garment worker in Montreal in 1974, Arnopoulos[18] earned 60 cents an hour and she reported the prevalence of illegal practices such as paying workers below the minimum wage and holding back payment for extra pieces. In 1982, a garment worker's hourly wage of $6.13 was 62 per cent of the hourly wage ($9.81) of all manufacturing industries.[19] In 1985, the average weekly earnings in the garment industry were only 55 per cent of the average earnings in all manufacturing industries.[20] In 1988, garment workers earned an hourly rate of about 66 per cent of what all manufacturing workers earned hourly.[21]

The working environments of shops and homeworkers have always been undesirable. In the late 19th century, workers used their bedrooms and living rooms as workrooms and similar arrangements are to be found within homework today. In almost every interview I conducted in my

1986 study[22] of garment workers in Toronto, respondents reported health and safety problems. These included both physical and mental stresses associated with piece work which resulted in insomnia, stomach ulcers and back pain.

## Role of the Canadian State

As the preceding discussion has already revealed, the Canadian state, more specifically the federal and provincial governments, has facilitated globalization, free trade, the rise of homework and thus a continuation of the super-exploitation of garment workers. In effect, government policies, regulations, practices and simple "neglect" in many instances have benefitted large, multinational enterprises, including the retail giants. Even in 1983, when employment was still rising in the garment industry, the president of the Manufacturers Association in Toronto said the following about the role of the government:

> the government is just starting to wake up … it is disinterested … it's against secondary industries and catering to high technology industries. It pays little attention to secondary industries which ordinary people depend on. Now may be too little and too late.[23]

Despite many protectionist measures, such as import quotas, the larger companies have continued to manoeuvre and access "cheap" labour through their global strategies.

Another policy used to rationalize the operations of garment and textile companies is a long-lasting government initiative. The Textile and Clothing Board (TCB), established in 1970, monitored the effects of imports, provided loan guarantees and encouraged the building of productivity centres. This policy of rationalization was more beneficial to larger companies because smaller companies generally lack access to investment capital necessary for new technology. Besides, the garment industry cannot be mechanized to a very high degree because of "short runs", i.e., the limited quantity of production and variety of production. Products are individually designed subject to the fashion industry, which experiences frequent changes in designs, seasonal fluctuations and changing consumer demands. Thus, standardization of products is low. Hence, investing money in highly automated machinery is impractical. Moreover, it is generally believed that mechanization programs are wasted unless there are effective import quotas.

The 1970 TCB was joined in 1981 by the Canadian Industrial Renewal Program (CIRP) which coordinated all adjustment assistance activities related to the textile and garment industries. Labour adjustment programs were financed by the Canada Employment and Immigration Commission and the TCB continued to advise the government regarding the impact of international trade on these industries. However, as in earlier years, the CIRP did not fundamentally change the vulnerability of the garment industry and it was still predominantly labour intensive. The TCB and the CIRP were terminated in 1986, at which point the Canadian International Trade Tribunal (CITT) was established.

Unions and homeworkers' advocacy organizations have pointed out the ineptness of laws such as the provincially-applied Employment Standards Acts (ESA) which theoretically provide minimum protection for non-unionized workers in Canada.[24] The ESA in Ontario excludes homeworkers who are providing services from home. Many employers like to argue that homeworkers are actually "self employed." If their argument is to be accepted, then it follows that homeworkers are not protected by the ESA. Therefore, definitions and language use have been used to exclude homeworkers from their rights as "workers."

Moreover, employers of homeworkers can easily deny their "employer" status since most of them are not registered with the government[25] and there is usually no pay slip attached to the wages with indications of employer deductions for Canada Pension Plan (CPP) and Unemployment Insurance (UIC). Therefore, there is no legal proof of the employer-employee relationship. Hence, if a homeworker were to file a complaint with the Employment Standards Branch (ESB), the onus is on her to prove that she is indeed a bona fide "employee." In addition, since homeworkers are at the bottom of a hierarchical chain of control, the retail companies and large garment manufacturers can deny any responsibility since technically and legally they may not appear to be "employing" them. The liability is shifted to the small manufacturer or the contractor in the middle who directly employs homeworkers.

Even if homeworkers are recognized as legitimate workers, under the ESA they are only protected by minimum wage and vacation pay provisions. Until December 1993, homeworkers in Ontario were not covered by maximum hours of work, overtime pay and statutory holidays. This small gain was made after intensive organizing and lobbying efforts by the Coalition for Fair Wages and Working Conditions for Homeworkers, an advocacy organization based in Toronto. In some of the provinces, homeworkers are still unprotected by these basic provisions won by Ontario homeworkers.

Nevertheless, even the few basic rights that they have are denied to homeworkers in practice because of the lack of enforcement mechanisms by the ESB as well as individual interpretations of the ESA. The Brief to the Ministry of Women's Equality[26] points out that there seems to be a contradiction between the "intention" of fairness and equity towards workers enshrined in the legislated act and the actual interpretation of it by government officials.

A 1993 brief[27] points out that neither the ESA nor the Industrial Standards Act, which regulates standards for garment workers in factories, enables inspectors to enter homes to investigate working conditions. The brief further points out that the ESA is based on a model of employees working in long-term, full-time positions with the same employer. It does not address the needs of homeworkers many of whom work for several employers at the same time and for short, irregular periods of time. Ocran et al[28] also confirm this point adding that the ESA does not benefit piece workers as it is designed for hourly waged workers.

It is easy to see how the lack of effective regulation of the labour market by the government, particularly in the garment industry, has encouraged the exploitation of homeworkers and factory workers. This situation has contributed to the reproduction of a specialized labour market which has been described as "captive."[29]

## Racialized and Gendered Working Class

Discrimination against garment workers, particularly those who work as homeworkers, is difficult to identify because it is seldom manifested in overt acts. In my interviews with workers, they frequently denied the experience of discrimination for a variety of reasons. What they experience is subtle, covert, and part of "everyday life". It is systemic. Systemic discrimination arises from conscious or unconscious policies, procedures and practices which adversely affect women and people of colour, such as their exclusion, segregation or elimination. Systemic discrimination is supported by institutional power and perpetuated over time.

Garment workers are subjected to systemic discrimination when their class status, immigration status, colour, language skills, gender and age are used to define them as the "other", render them "invisible" and exclude them from regular, mainstream institutional opportunities. Additionally, systemic discrimination can be used to segregate garment workers into a "captive" labour market marked by super-exploitive characteristics. Often the "otherization" of garment workers is expressed in daily discourse by referring to *all* garment workers as "immigrant women" or by identifying the industry as "an industry of immigrant women." Although I am not aware of any studies documenting the citizenship status of garment workers, I would argue that most of them are actually "Canadian citizens," although they are not Canadian-born, and came as immigrants and refugees. To identify racism and sexism experienced by these workers, I have relied upon a variety of methods, namely institutional analysis, employment systems analysis and, of course, personal interviews.

As mentioned, garment sector jobs are generally low-paid, lacking in promotional opportunities, non-unionized, labelled as "unskilled" and generally insecure. New immigrant women, non-English-speaking women, and women of colour are the prime candidates for these jobs, accounting for 76.7 per cent of the total number of garment workers.[30] I am not aware of any accounts of the racial and ethnic composition of the garment industry in the 19th and 20th centuries. In general, the ethnic and racial make-up of the garment labour force is largely conditioned by the nature of immigration policies in Canada.

For example the Retirees' Club of the International Ladies Garment Workers Union (ILGWU), [whose members consisted of male workers who had been active in the labour force in the 1930s], were all Eastern European Jewish Canadians. A report[31] from the 1920s confirms that the largest ethnic group in the Quebec garment industry was Jewish. There were also some Italians, Ukrainians, Poles, other immigrants and French-Canadians in the country shops. The predominance of Jewish people in the industry was a reflection of the migration of Eastern European Jews to Canada between 1880 and 1920 after being displaced from professional and educational work due to anti-Semitism and the rise of industrial capitalism in Europe.

Arnopoulos reported in 1974 that most of the shops she visited in Montreal had workers from Southern Europe and Third World countries.[32] My research in the Toronto garment industry in the 1980s[33] revealed that marker-makers, graders, cutters, and pressers were white European men, some being Jewish, with rare occurrences of South Asian men, while sewing machine operators and finishers were primarily women of Portuguese and Italian origins. Men and women of colour appeared to predominate in non-union shops. For example, I encountered a large non-unionized factory where workers, many of them senior citizens, were predominantly from the Punjab. I also saw a significant number of women of East Asian origin who were sewing machine operators. Gannage's[34] study conducted in Toronto in the 1980s also revealed the predominance of Jewish, Eastern European and Southern European garment workers. The ILGWU's study of the Great Sewing Exchange in Toronto, a factory established in 1982, stated that the main language groups among workers were English, Italian, Portuguese and Cantonese.[35] This pattern is confirmed by a 1981 report that said that 51 per cent of sewing machine operators in Canada were born in Southern Europe and 26 per cent were born in Asia.[36]

A 1985 Report[37] said that 46.9 per cent of all women garment workers and 43.7 per cent of all men garment workers were born outside Canada, and of these 14.7 per cent were Southern Europeans and 11.8 per cent were Asians. Forty-one percent claimed a first language other than English or French. The proportion of Southern European women in garment work fell from 24.2 per cent in 1981 to 21.0 per cent in 1986. During the same period, the proportion of Asian-born women had increased from 11.8 per cent to 16.3 per cent. This is an indication of immigration trends in Canada in recent years, where a larger proportion is originating in Asia than in Europe. Chinese-Canadian women are three times more likely to be found in product fabrication than other women workers and they work primarily as sewing machine operators in the garment industry.[38] It has been reported that 94 per cent of sewing machine operators in Toronto today are born outside Canada.[39] Seward points out that a higher proportion of garment workers in Ontario are born outside Canada than in Quebec.[40]

It is crucial to note that the intrinsic characteristics of immigrants and people of colour are not responsible for the deplorable labour conditions in the garment industry. Their low political status, as defined by their immigration status, their "racial visibility", their "linguistic visibility", their gender and their lack of union protection make them perfect recruits to this sector. Their "cheap" labour is predicated on this political vulnerability. It is in the social and political organization of this vulnerability that racism, sexism and classism occurs.

Working class women with landed immigrant or refugee status face legal and structural barriers to entering "mainstream" institutions, whether in the private or public sectors. Canada's new immigrants are increasingly non-English and non-French speaking. In 1986, for example, 42 per cent of immigrants were in this category.[41] By the 1980s, two out of three immigrants came from Africa, Asia, the Caribbean, and Central and South America.[42] Women immigrants are more likely to be without one of the official Canadian languages. The first language of three-quarters of Chinese-Canadian women is neither English nor French.[43] Without the use of an official language, and lacking access to subsidized English-as-Second-Language (ESL) classes, these women remain marginalized and destined to job "ghettoes."

Language classes are now provided by two federal programs known as LINC (Language Instruction for Newcomers to Canada) and LMLT (Labour Market Language Training), both introduced in January 1992. Immigrant agencies, the labour movement and community-based training advocates[44] have critiqued these programs as being inaccessible to most immigrants. For instance, LINC programs are not available to those who are Canadian citizens or to refugee claimants. Since many people who do not speak English or French are citizens of Canada, they are ineligible for LINC classes. Moreover, LINC classes are not geared to employment or skill training. LMLT programs are available to citizens but only for those whose occupations are deemed to be in demand locally. Besides there is no easy transition from LINC to LMLT classes. As Lior comments, "there is a gap between the end of LINC and the lowest level of LMLT."[45] Moreover, training allowances are not consistently available for those who take these programs. In 1993-94, 55 per cent of trainees did not receive an allowance. The lack of a training allowance acts as a strong disincentive to taking ESL classes. Childcare provisions are inadequate as only "childminding" is provided rather than good quality childcare governed by provincial standards. Educators and advocates have also been critical of the curriculum and pedagogic approaches of LINC and LMLT programs. One person commented that "when a person graduates from LINC, they have not learnt the language by any means."[46] This is corroborated by a brief[47] which states that after finishing LINC level three, "the level of language ability acquired by learners is insufficient to allow them to function independently in society."

Before LINC and LMLT, federally-sponsored ESL classes were not accessible to most immigrant women since priority was placed on making them available to immigrant "breadwinners", mostly assumed by immigration authorities to be the men of the household.[48] Historically, most immigrant women have entered Canada under the "family class" or "assisted relative class" section. Both categories are sponsored by "independent" immigrants. Immigration authorities and policymakers assume that sponsored immigrants are not destined to the labour market, nor are they "employable." This stereotype, which is part of a sexist ideology, continues today despite statistics which show that the labour force participation of immigrant women is higher than that of Canadian-born women. Estable and Meyer[49] documented that Canada Employment Centres (CECs) generally provide information to the male immigrants and assume that it will "trickle" down to their female relatives. It has also been documented that CEC counsellors will try to channel immigrant women towards stereotypical jobs, as these are accessible without knowledge of either official language. Furthermore, if the woman is judged to be "employable" without training and ESL classes, she is effectively barred from learning either official language. Thus, women who are long-time residents of Canada may still be unable to communicate with the larger society. In 1986, Employment and Immigration estimated that over 90,000 immigrants from the period 1980 to 1984 still required language classes.[50] A significant proportion of Southern European Canadian women in the garment industry have no knowledge of either official language, even though 85 per cent of them have been in Canada for 10 to 30 years.[51] Learning either of the official languages is not a pre-requisite for the garment industry. Nor are the workers able to gain fluency on the job since they probably rely on their native tongues for job communication. Without fluency in one of the official languages, a woman cannot enter any training programs at post-secondary institutions. Thus, her chances for a better job are practically nil.

Immigration criteria have made it virtually impossible for women to apply as "independent" immigrants. Among other criteria, Canada emphasizes official language skill, eligibility for jobs in demand in Canada, education and ownership of capital, in assessing applicants. Working class women, worldwide, cannot fulfill these requirements, given the entrenched sexism and class relations in most societies. Ironically, women have had to resort to the Live-in Caregiver Program (previously known as Foreign Domestic Movement) in order to work in Canada. However, even these programs are becoming more restrictive as more exclusive criteria are implemented. For example, domestic workers are now required to have grade 13 and formal training. This means that working class women from Third World countries will have a harder time fulfilling the requirements. As has been well documented,[52] these "special" programs are ways of legalizing and maintaining captive labour forces to supply the labour needs in areas where White, Canadian-born women would rarely work. These programs are administered in such a way that if the contracted women violate any of the immigration and employment conditions they can be deported.

The reason people continue to immigrate to Canada under such restrictive conditions is connected to colonization, imperialism and globalization, and the resulting distortion of economic, social and political development faced by Third World countries. Despite the fact that a large proportion of immigrant men and women these days have professional and post-secondary education (14.4 per cent of immigrants had university degrees in 1991 compared to 10.5 per cent of Canadian-born),[53] most, particularly those from Third World countries, experience devaluation of qualifications and work experience from their original countries. Although immigrant women are more likely to be university educated than Canadian-born women, they are less likely to be in a professional job.[54] Many professionals, such as teachers and doctors, are asked to upgrade, re-enter universities, and some have been advised to take up training in an unrelated, relatively low-skilled area. Although the level of education of workers in the garment industry is much lower overall than workers in manufacturing, the case of Asian women workers is interesting. While a large proportion of Asian workers have less than grade five education, a higher proportion of them also have grades 11 to 13 and university education compared to the overall population of women workers in the industry.[55] Cameron and Mak[56] said that two out of 30 Chinese homeworkers interviewed had professional training, in nursing and in law respectively. Four out of six South Asian homeworkers I interviewed have technical training or a Bachelor of Arts education. About 40 per cent of Spanish-speaking homeworkers interviewed have professional qualifications from their countries of origin. One woman I interviewed doing own account[57] sewing has a Masters of Arts from Pakistan in a professional field, but has been assessed as having a grade 13 in Canada. The experience of most non-English or French speaking working class people of colour who originally entered the country as immigrants and refugees is that they remain a marginalized group in all sectors of society; a group which remains "visible" by their "invisibility" and "marginality" and forever seen as "immigrant" and "foreign".

As mentioned, the "immigrant" adjective may be a perceived notion rather than a real or legal one for most garment workers, as immigrants can apply for Canadian citizenship after three years of residency in the country. Why, then, are garment workers all lumped in under the category "immigrant"? In Canada, the term "immigrant" is often used interchangeably with "ethno-racial minorities" or "people of colour" at an everyday level.[58] This everyday, "commonsense" equation hides a racialized concept of who a "true Canadian" is and what "real Canadian culture" resembles. A person in Canadian society is described as a "Canadian" or an "immigrant" at a "commonsense" level depending on their physical characteristics, dress, headgear or English or French skills. Therefore, garment workers, predominantly non-English-speaking women of colour not born in Canada, are seen as "non-Canadian", as "outsiders", as people who "do not want to assimilate into Canadian culture". This "non-Canadian-ness", this apparent "unassimilability" and this outsider status is socially, politically and economically constructed by various institutional processes, beyond those within the garment industry itself.

Unlike white, Canadian-born women with knowledge of one of the official languages, women of colour and non-English-speaking women within the garment industry have no security, no promotions, earn super-exploitative wages often paid by the piece, and work in unsafe health conditions. Unlike white, Canadian-born women, these women are "stuck" in a "captive" labour force due to structural and institutional practices.

These practices operate within a larger capitalist dynamic of crises, "glo-balization," and an emphasis on disempowerment and "cheapening" la-bour.

The vulnerability of the garment industry in recent years, is character-ized by plant closures and the rise of homework. Middle-aged women without one of the official languages and with low educational back-grounds have been most adversely affected by rising unemployment due to plant closures. A study[59] of plant closures revealed that 80 per cent of the men unemployed in manufacturing industries found jobs in their field, whereas only 38 per cent of women did so. Retraining was a difficult option for many workers because of pre-requisites of grade 10 education, English and Math skills and qualifying tests which are often culturally bi-ased. Seward[60] estimates that about 54 per cent of garment workers have less than grade 10 education. Re-training often does not build on "old" skills. Moreover, there is a long waiting list for re-training programs and a requirement of being a Canadian resident for one year or more.

The rise of homework has adversely affected immigrant women and women of colour who were already working in garment factories. The tasks which have been removed from the factory floor to the home have predominantly been sewing and finishing, mainly performed by non-English-speaking women and women of colour. Racial segmentation was always an intrinsic characteristic of the labour process in this industry, and continues today. Whereas women and men were previously segre-gated on the shop floor, divided by space, walls and by language barriers, most women are now doing paid work in their homes. Thus, the segrega-tion is complete – there is almost no chance of interaction with other workers, and, indeed, with any adults other than one's own relatives and friends. Shops using contractors and homeworkers retain the skilled workers, who have historically been predominantly male and White. Ironically, the lack of contact with adults from the external world is some-times seen as an advantage by homeworkers who want to avoid "bosses" and overt racism at all cost.[61]

Employment dynamics within the garment industry also maintain the gendered and racialized labour markets, as the following examples show.

*Recruitment*: Hiring is predominantly done by "word of mouth", i.e., a friend, an aunt, a sister or a brother says there is work available. Since word of mouth relies on familial and ethnic networks, ethnicity, gender and race are reproduced systemically. The hiring is informal, with minimal paperwork, no interviews and no open competitions in the traditional sense. In this process, it is almost impossible to break the established norms of segregation. The following are some testimonies:

"When I came to Canada, I had a hard time. I was 21 years old. I married. I don't know English. I asked my husband's friend's wife. She informed me about job."

"I was hired by the boss. She worked with me in another place. She came to supervise me in this factory. She asked some of the girls to come with her."

"My brother-in-law was making nice and expensive coats in a factory. Very nice job, but it was hard for me to understand English. I was tall and skinny. They used me as a model."[62]

Since the word-of-mouth method is the most common technique of hiring workers in this industry, shops are ethnically and racially homogenous, relatively speaking. This suits Canadians who lack fluency in one of the official languages. However, one can imagine the difficulty faced by applicants whose ethnicity or race is in the minority in any particular shop. Perhaps this explains the lack of Black or South Asians in shops where Southern Europeans or Chinese workers are in the majority. On the other hand, as mentioned earlier, there was one factory I encountered where workers were predominantly South Asian. Black workers in this industry are almost non-existent, which I believe may be an indication of a racialized, sexist stereotyping emanating from slavery in the Americas in which Black women are generally expected to perform physically heavy jobs in a way which defies standards of White, European or Asian femininity. Black women are also seen as nurturing in an intuitive way, but not passive. The long history of Black women's resistance to slavery and racism has typecast them as "rebellious." Within this racist paradigm they are not seen to be suited to the meticulous, precise and repetitive work garment making entails. Asian and European women, on the other hand, are more stereotyped as being suited to this kind of work. Therefore, it appears that gender ideologies are racially mediated.

The other method of hiring that workers mentioned was through the union, the ILGWU. Unemployed garment workers who are union members from previous work experiences can be referred to union shops that are hiring new workers. This leaves out non-members who are largely immigrant workers and more likely to be people of colour. However, since the industry has been rapidly declining over the past few years, it is unlikely that this mode of hiring is used frequently.

*Promotions*: There are no promotional opportunities to speak of. One worker said: "Promotions are given after six months. Ladies get 10 cents, men get 15 cents. There's no system. They give to everyone. They give Italian more, more to White, they do this. They give less to older workers."[63]

The above testimony notes that promotions are equated with wage increments, rather than with changing jobs. On the technical ladder of "skills", workers, particularly piece workers, can never learn "tailoring", i.e., the combined abilities to design, cut and sew the entire garment. Neither is there any need for tailors in this industry because of the deskilling and degradation of garment-making itself over the 19th and 20th centuries. Therefore, training for garment workers is virtually nil. This is even more so for piece workers, most of whom work on specialized machines, (which, in effect, embody skills that workers held in the past).

Occasionally, one might encounter someone who "moved" from a sewing position to being a designer or a supervisor. But these are rare exceptions and based on subjective management decisions. When they happen, it is usually a case where a supervisor takes a "special liking" to a particular worker. I have yet to encounter a supervisor who is a person of colour. For example, in the factory where workers were predominantly South Asian, the supervisor was a White, Jewish man.

*Termination*: Garment workers can be terminated overnight, particularly if they are non-unionized. Getting fired, like being hired, is informal and subjective. Besides, workers who are outspoken or active in the union are often targeted for quick dismissals. The following are some testimonies on arbitrary firings:

"If she's no good, she can get fired. Maybe business is slow – the bad ones laid off first, good ones last. Maybe for fighting."

"The way the bosses want it, they do it (firing). I had an argument. I worked for pennies for 25 years. A couple of days back they give me a note to terminate me. Two days later, they asked me to forget it. But who knows? There's not much work. They've got an excuse to fire me."[64]

Given the characteristics of the industry, particularly while it is in its current phase of globalization, factories seem to be closing by leaps and bounds as employers seek to maximize their profits by moving to "cheap labour" zones either in so-called Third World countries or by employing women of colour as homeworkers here in Canada. Workplaces which run on the subjective whims of supervisors or employers are prone to biased employment systems. Since there is almost no standardization, personal prejudices and stereotypes on the basis of sex, ethnicity, race and age can bias labour-management relations.

*Climate*: The climate depends on the particular shop being looked at, its size and the level of militancy of workers. Some worker testimonies show that feelings of prejudice against different ethnic or racial groups exist, although in a mild and subterranean form. They take the forms of namecalling, jokes and stereotypes. One South Asian male cutter interviewed said:

"Portuguese and Italian ladies steal a lot.... They do business outside.... They sell...."[65]

An Italian woman worker said:

"A coloured girl objected because we talk in Italian and she can't understand what we talk in the union. She is an underpresser. She wants to go back to school. She came only once to the picket line.... The Chinese don't come, Portuguese women don't come, Pakistanis don't come. Only Italians and Greeks come to the picketline."[66]

Moreover, some workers expressed anti-Semitic feelings. A White, non-Jewish man said:

"English shop is easier, Jewish is rough. English people are quiet, never yell."[67]

"He (owner) was hardly around. He couldn't care a damn. He was a Jew."[68]

Anti-management feelings and anti-Semitism are rolled into one in the above testimony.

The employment systems described for factory workers in the garment industry are more or less true for homeworkers also. However, in the latter case, employment is so precarious that employers or contractors have the liberty to be completely arbitrary in terms of the regularity and frequency of "supplying work". The line between hiring and firing is so thin that they can hardly be differentiated by the workers themselves. The following is one testimony of a homeworker:

"I call and tell him I need work. He doesn't call me until there is more work."[69]

Despite the illusion of being protected in the sanctity of one's home, the isolation of homeworkers spells out loss of control. It signifies deunionization, the lack of solidarity from other workers in the same predicament and a lack of a political voice. It is a systemic mechanism for invisibility and disempowerment. Ocran et al[70] have argued that this invisibility is an asset for employers who want to conduct their business under the table. Conversely, this invisibility and illegality prevents homeworkers from asserting their rights because it may mean losing their jobs and, in some cases, their residency in Canada. Confined to their homes, women of colour who are homeworkers continue to be stigmatized as "immigrant women" and as "dependent housewives and mothers," who are really "not workers."

## Racism and Sexism on the Shopfloor

*Segregation*: Task groups in garment shops are frequently differentiated by sex, race and ethnicity. There are often wage gradations between them to further exacerbate the difference. The diagram is an aerial view of one shop I encountered in my research.[71]

The underpressers in the top left corner were predominantly Southern European men, the button-hole makers were women of colour, one Black and the other South Asian. On the top right corner were two groups of

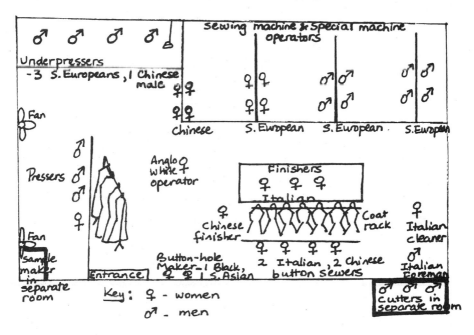

four operators, each older, White European men. To the left, there was another group of four operators who were White Southern European women. Further to their left was yet another group of four operators, who were Chinese women. Then below these 16 operators, there was a group of three Italian women finishers. There was one Canadian-born White, Anglo woman operator, one Chinese-speaking woman finisher and one Italian woman cleaner each working alone. The only mixed grouping was in the bottom right hand corner, where there were two Italian women and two women of Chinese origin working as button sewers. When questioned about worker interactions, one Eastern European male who works as a sewing machine operator said:

> "Immigrants are different in background ... different culture ... different custom. To bring this together takes half your life.... They stick together. I'm Jewish. I can't speak Chinese. What will I speak to them? What do I have in common with them? I would like to speak to them...."[72]

Communication between task groups is often thwarted by the lack of a common language in a shop such as the one described above. Ocran et al[73] have noted that there are linguistic connections to specific types of homework in Lower Mainland B.C. For example, Vietnamese-speaking homeworkers are often knitters, while Punjabi-speaking homeworkers are sewing machine operators. In Toronto, it appears that Chinese-speaking homeworkers predominate in sewing, while "own account" food production is more prevalent among South Asian women. Garment sewing work may be associated with Asian women, as racial stereotypes suggest they have "nimble fingers."

There also seems to be a pattern in the ethnic composition of garment workforces based on the location of the factories in Toronto. Those closer to the city of Toronto are made up of the older, Eastern European, Jewish and Southern European workers. As the factories spread out into the suburbs of Mississauga and Malton, the workforces consist of workers of colour. Perhaps this reflects the residence patterns of newer immigrant groups in the metropolitan Toronto area.

*Bias in Work Allocation*: There are some indications of biases in work allocation among garment workers. A Chinese sewing machine operator said the following:

"Mr.____ on King St. tested me on machine. I cried and cried because I don't know English. I went to night school. Sometimes the forelady gave me the bundle. I didn't understand. I got 18 cents for one bundle ... the Black girl took the good bundle. She knew I didn't know English."

This testimony reveals that the Chinese worker perceived that she was discriminated against because she is not fluent in English. She was given a less desired "bundle", which presumably results in lower earnings. Ironically, the worker who got the "good" bundle was a Black woman, according to the Chinese worker. She also reveals a level of racialization when she refers to her competitor as a "black girl" rather than simply a "girl". Another worker of colour said this to emphasize bias in work allocation:

"if there is a Chinese supervisor, she will give more work to Chinese workers and less to Italians, East Indians...."[74]

"I started work before Marguerita. She has guts and so she is on time work. I'm still on piece work. I work more than her. She doesn't work better than me. She earns more than me. Maybe she's white, that's why they pay more to her."[75]

Racial or ethnic affinity was frequently mentioned as an underlying cause of biased work allocation. However, I also found that in situations of labour-management conflict, for instance during strikes or unionization drives, ethnic affinity can easily change to vicious harassment. Racial and ethnic affinity leading to biased work allocation may be an indication that "one's own kind" is more competent or trustworthy, and therefore preferred over workers who are "foreign". Apart from these assumptions, biased work allocation also promotes competition and breaks worker solidarity.

*Infantalization*: The reference to *all* female garment workers as "girls" without heed to their age, is an indication of infantalization. This is a manifestation of patriarchal ideology where women are seen as being like children, still in their developmental process prior to adulthood, in need of supervision, protection and disciplining by men. Men are seen in this ideology as the opposite of women, i.e., adult, independent, capable and having the authority to supervise, protect and discipline women and children. As discussed earlier, the "ward" status of most immigrant women and women of colour is formally reproduced through the immigration process and the orchestration of processes from other institutions to which these women have contact.

Some workers clearly indicated differential pay to "newer" immigrant workers, usually women of colour, who were perceived to be unskilled, inexperienced, and financially and legally more vulnerable than "older" immigrant workers who are usually White and skilled. The following are some comments by them:

"Before, all the Jewish men were machinists. Women are cheaper as machinists. Women do section work – back sleeves. They are cheaper. They are all piece workers."[76]

"Cutters today are not Jewish. They get paid less. The Korean people got into the trade. They got $6 an hour. Someone born here won't work for that money. From the price of me and ___, they can get four. They (new cutters) are not skilled. They can't make markers. They can't speak English. They can't ask for anything more. That's the advantage bosses have. They (new cutters) come over in a boat and don't speak English. They start at a low wage...."[77]

Management and some White workers are participating in a process of infantalizing, in which new workers, who are more likely to be people of colour, women and newly arrived immigrants, are stereotyped and prejudged as "not good enough". The devaluation of their labour rationalizes the fact that employers pay them much less for the same or similar tasks. In the process, the dignity, self worth and adulthood of these immigrant workers are reduced. Older, White, male workers often express a resentment towards newer workers for "lowering standards." The following comment was made by a Portuguese-Canadian woman who was a garment worker but who had been unemployed as a result of her factory shutting down:

"Chinese workers are accepting lower wages and we're forced to take lower wages. We cannot afford that because we have houses and mortgages to pay."[78]

It is significant to note that this comment was made in the presence of her colleague who was a Chinese-Canadian woman. When her comment was critiqued by my informant, he said:

"It became a full-blown argument. She then proceeded to scapegoat welfare recipients, refugees, immigrants and teenagers."

My informant tells me that the woman did not show up for her appointment on the following day. Her characterization of "Chinese workers" as working for lower wages and juxtaposing that with "we ... have mortgages to pay" implies that Chinese-Canadians do not buy houses, do not have trouble with low wages or with poverty in general. This subtle comparison brings to mind one of the many stereotypes emanating from orientalism, associated with "the Chinese" at the turn of the century, namely that "they" are accustomed to low pay.

## Notes

1. For more details of the research process, see Tania Das Gupta, *Degradation and Deskilling*, p.163-172.
2. Michael M. Hart, *Canadian Economic Development and the International Trading System* (Toronto: University of Toronto Press, 1985), p. 109.
3. Rianne Mahon, "Canadian Labour in the Battle of the Eighties," *Studies in Political Economy* (Summer, 1983), p. 157.
4. ILGWU, "General Executive Board Report to the 40th Convention of the ILGWU," June, 1989, p. 23.
5. "The Global Garment Industry: Industrial Model of the Future," *Economic Justice Report*, V, 1 (April 1994), p.3.
6. International Ladies Garment Workers Union (ILGWU), *The Race to the Bottom: Brief Presented to the Government of Ontario Special Committee on the NAFTA*, Toronto, April 8, 1993.
7. Tania Das Gupta, *Degradation and Deskilling: the Case of the Garment Industry in Toronto*, PhD Thesis, University of Toronto, 1986, p. 259.
8. Carla Lipsig-Mumme, "Organizing Women in the Clothing Trades: Homework and the 1983 Garment Strike in Canada," *Studies in Political Economy*, 22 (Spring 1987), p.41-71.
9. ILGWU, *The Race*, p. 2.
10. Amanda Ocran, Jennifer Hyndman, Natalie Jamieson, *Industrial Homework and Employment Standards: A Community Approach to Visibility and Understanding, A Brief for Improved Employment Legislation for the Ministry of Women's Equality*, (Vancouver: The Women and Work Research and Education Society and ILGWU, 1993), p.1.
11. Barbara Cameron and Teresa Mak, "Working Conditions of Chinese Speaking Homeworkers in the Toronto Garment Industry: Summary of the Results of a Survey Conducted by the ILGWU," Toronto, 1991.
12. Jan Borowoy and Fanny Yuen, "ILGWU 1993 Homeworkers' Study: Summary of Study Findings," Toronto, 1993, p.5.
13. Economic Justice Report, *The Global*, p.5.
14. Ibid, p.5.
15. ILGWU, *The Race*, p.17.
16. For details on historical trends in wages, hours of work, conditions of work etc., see Tania Das Gupta, *Degradation and Deskilling*, pp.196-255.
17. Laura C. Johnson, *The Seam Allowance* (Toronto: The Women's Press, 1982), p.75.
18. Refer to Irving Abella and David Millar, *The Canadian Worker in the Twentieth Century* (Toronto: Oxford University Press, 1978).
19. Reported in Das Gupta, *Degradation and Deskilling*, p.227.
20. Shana Wong, "Issues Facing Asian Canadian Women," Chinese Canadian National Council, Toronto, 1991.
21. ILGWU, "General Executive Board Report to the 40th Convention of the ILGWU," June, 1989, p. 22.

22. Das Gupta, *Degradation and Deskilling*.

23. Das Gupta, *Degradation and Deskilling*, p.202.

24. ILGWU, *Race To the Bottom*; Ocran et al, *Industrial Homework*.

25. Borowoy and Yuen,*1993 Homeworkers' Study*.

26. Ocran et al, *Industrial Homework*, p.20.

27. ILGWU and Intercede, *The Race*, p. 21.

28. Ocran et al, *Industrial Homework*, p.2.

29. Roxana Ng and Tania Das Gupta, "Nation-Builders? The Captive Labour Force of Non-English-Speaking Immigrant Women," *Canadian Women's Studies*, Vol 3, No. 1 (1981), p. 83-89.

30. Shirley B. Seward, ""Challenges of Labour Adjustment: the Case of Immigrant Women in the Clothing Industry," Studies in Social Policy, Ottawa, March 1990, p. 9.

31. Abella and Millar, *Canadian Worker*.

32. Abella and Millar, *Canadian Worker*, p. 203.

33. Das Gupta, *Deskilling and Degradation*.

34. Charlene Gannage, *Double Day Double Bind* (Toronto: The Women's Press, 1986).

35. ILGWU, *When One Door Closes...Another One Opens? A Follow-Up Study on the Closure of the Great Sewing Exchange* (Toronto: ILGWU, June 1994), p.2.

36. Shana Wong, "Issues Facing Asian Canadian Women,"Chinese Canadian National Council, Toronto, 1991.

37. *Women in Industry: North-South Connections* (Canada: The North-South Institute, 1985).

38. Patricia Lee, "Chinese-Canadian Women: A Demographic Profile," Chinese Canadian National Council, Toronto, March, 1992.

39. ILGWU, *The Race*, p.2.

40. Seward,"Challenges," p. 9.

41. Alma Estable and Mechthild Meyer, *A Discussion Paper on Settlement Needs of Immigrant Women in Ontario,Immigrant Settlement and Adaptation Program*, CEIC, Toronto, March 1989, p.19.

42. Multiculturalism and Citizenship Canada,*Multiculturalism: What Is It Really About?* (Canada: Ministry of Supply and Services, 1991), p.31.

43. Lee, "Chinese Canadian Women," p. 2.

44. Karen Lior, "Briefing Notes: Federal Language Training Policy," Toronto, undated.

45. Karen Lior, "LINC To What?" *Women's Education des Femme*, Vol. 10, No. 3-4 (Winter, 1993/94).

46. Lior, "LINC To What?"

47. Ontario Council of Agencies Serving Immigrants, "LINC Community Recommendations," Submission to The Honourable Bernard Valcourt, Minister of Employment and Immigration, June, 1993, p.4.

48. Estable and Mayer, *Discussion Paper*, p.20.

49. Ibid, p. 47.

50. Ibid, p.20.
51. Seward, "Challenges of Labour Adjustment," p. 10.
52. Patricia Daenzer, *Regulating Class Privilege: Immigrant Servants in Canada, 1940's-1990's* (Toronto: Canadian Scholars' Press, 1993); Agnes Calliste, "Canada's Immigration Policy and Domestics From the Caribbean: The Second Domestic Scheme," in Jesse Vorst, Tania Das Gupta et al (eds.) *Race, Class, Gender: Bonds and Barriers* (Winnipeg: Society for Socialist Studies, 1991); ILGWU and Intercede, *The Race.*
53. "Immigrants An Asset," *Toronto Star*, July 14, 1994, p. A24.
54. Estable and Mayer, *Discussion Paper*, p.23.
55. Seward, "Challenges," p.10.
56. Barbara Cameron and Teresa Mak, "Working Conditions of Chinese Speaking Homeworkers in the Toronto Garment Industry: Summary of the Results of a Survey Conducted By the ILGWU," Toronto, 1991, p.5.
57. "Own account" self employed workers are those who are hired directly by an employer or client for a service or a commodity for an agreed upon amount of money. They retain a fair amount of control over their own labour process although they may not be earning a high income. For more discussion on this group of workers, see Tania Das Gupta, "Globalization and Domestication: Two Sides of the Same Coin," Unpublished Paper, York University, September, 1994, p. 5.
58. This is clearly captured in testimonies gathered in Carl E. James, *Seeing Ourselves: Exploring Race, Ethnicity and Culture*, (Toronto: Thompson Educational Publishing, Inc.,1995), p. 25, 52, 170, 175.
59. Kathy Jones and Valerie Huff, "Plant Closure," *Our Times*, Vol.8, No. 1 (1989), p.22-25.
60. Seward, "Challenges of Labour Adjustment,"p.10.
61. Ocran et al, *Industrial Homework*, p. 15; Swasti Mitter, *Common Fate, Common Bond: Women in the Global Economy* (London: Pluto Press, 1986), p. 130.
62. Das Gupta, *Degradation and Deskilling*, p. 311.
63. Das Gupta, *Degradation*, p. 318.
64. Das Gupta, *Degradation*, p. 318.
65. Ibid, p. 303.
66. Ibid, p. 372.
67. Ibid, p.372.
68. Ibid, p. 373.
69. Homeworker R, Interviewed on July 20, 1994, Toronto.
70. Ocran et al, *Industrial Homework*.
71. Das Gupta, *Degradation and Deskilling*, p.294.
72. Ibid, p.297.
73. Ocran et al, *Industrial Homework*.
74. Das Gupta, *Deskilling*, p. 325.
75. Ibid, p. 327.
76. Ibid, p. 338.

77. Ibid, p. 341.
78. Personal communication by Tariq Kidwai, who was working as a counsellor at the School of Labour at George Brown College in Toronto, June 23, 1995.

# Chapter 4

# Racism in Nursing

## Introduction and Research Methods

THIS CHAPTER describes and analyzes the existence of racism in nursing, revealing consistent patterns of covert and overt forms of racism faced by Black nurses in Ontario.

Research on racism in nursing is sparse, even though analyses of gender, sexism and class in this profession are more readily available.[1] I will explore systemic practices of racism as well as document the "everyday culture" of racism in hospitals, particularly in reference to Black female nurses. Even though I dwell on the experience and practices of racism in general, in particular I examine the experiences of women and members of the middle or professional class. I will comment on sexist racism which is apparent in daily interactions between Black nurses and their managers. Therefore, racism, gender and class will all be examined.

The experiences of Black nurses and other healthcare workers illustrate the various forms of racism discussed earlier. In the 1950s, Black women from the Caribbean were granted temporary entry permits to Canada in order to be trained as nursing assistants, and employed in "such unattractive specialties as psychiatric hospitals and sanatoria."[2] A study by Wilson Head[3] reveals that women of colour working in healthcare today are mostly concentrated at the lower levels of nursing, in cooking, cleaning and laundering, and thus create a racially-segmented workforce. There are very few nurses of colour at the supervisory level. Essed[4] also documents racial segregation in nursing in The Netherlands whereby Black nurses are over-represented in non-management positions, in geriatric nursing training, as home helpers and "temps". Lee-Cunin[5] confirms this pattern by saying that Black nurses in Britain are over-represented in areas where promotional opportunities are extremely limited, for example in geriatrics and psychiatry.

Workers of colour have been excluded from better paid, secure, and more desirable jobs in nursing through systemic practices in the labour market and in other related institutions, such as the educational and immigration systems. Calliste[6] writes that Canadian nursing schools did not admit Canadian-born Black students before the 1940s, apparently because Canadian hospitals would not employ them. It was only after a public campaign against this racist, sexist exclusion was conducted by the Nova Scotia Association for the Advancement of Coloured People and supported by some trade unions and church groups that this policy was challenged. Interestingly, Caribbean students were admitted into nursing schools because the assumption was that they would return to their countries of origin for employment.

Calliste writes that between 1950 and 1962, Canadian immigration authorities admitted limited numbers of Caribbean nurses, urged by groups such as the Negro Citizenship Association. However, they were admitted under differential rules compared to White nurse immigrants. Calliste argues that Black nurses "were required to have nursing 'qualifications over and above' those required for white nurses."[7] Out of the four categories of nurses accepted, one included graduate nurses from the Caribbean as students who were required to finish a three-month obstetrics course, be eligible for registration with the Registered Nurses Association as well as guaranteed employment by a hospital which was "aware of their racial origin". This is a significant point because Canadian hospitals had a "White only staffing" policy at that time. Upon fulfillment of all these requirements, they could apply for landed immigration status. In contrast, White nurse applicants without the obstetrics course were granted landed immigrant status by Order-in-Council. Moreover, some graduate nurses from the Caribbean worked as nursing assistants while waiting for entry into the obstetrics program because access to these courses for foreign students was limited. Another category of Black students was given temporary entry permits to enroll in nursing assistant programs offered by hospitals, provided there was a demand for them in these hospitals upon graduation. However, Calliste notes that only some of these graduates gained landed immigrant status whilst others continued on temporary work permits.

Lee-Cunin[8] notes how nursing schools in Britain are inaccessible to women of colour, and how reluctant they are to accommodate a change in nurse uniforms, for example, the right for Muslim nurses to wear trousers. Both of these factors have contributed to a decline in the recruitment of Black and Asian nurses at the time of research. Re-grading of nurses also led to the downgrading and underpayment of Black nurses.

Canadian research has revealed that, once hired by hospitals, nurses of colour are subjected to racially-biased performance appraisals or *no* documentation of their performance appraisals, which then disqualifies them from promotions. In the early 1960s, Black nurses with "better qualifications" than White nurses were discriminated against in terms of promotions purely on the basis of racism.[9] In Head's[10] study, the failure rate in promotions was significantly higher for Blacks than for Whites. Many of the Black professionals interviewed, including doctors, clearly attributed this to differential opportunities and to racism. Some talked about being "by-passed" or being told they were "too experienced."[11] Most Black workers felt their qualifications were not being utilized in their jobs, while most White workers felt the opposite. Stereotypes, prejudices, individual discrimination and systemic discrimination are not mutually exclusive. In fact, they are mutually reinforcing and occur as a continuous cultural process.

The Head[12] report documented Black workers being summarily dismissed and unjustly laid-off, healthcare institutions being unable to deal with complaints against Black workers, and those same workers being penalized for disagreeing with their supervisors.

Registered nurses are highly-skilled professionals, given a great deal of discretion and control, unionized, and in most cases well paid. They are not usually considered victims of exploitation and racial oppression in Canada. However, even within this middle-class group, we find evidence of intense and damaging racism, sexism, classism and ageism. Harassment is often the price one has to pay in order to challenge class privilege, which is almost always tied in with white skin and gender privileges. Essed[13] documents the insubordination of Black (Surinamese) nurse supervisors in The Netherlands. Essed[14] tells us that the harassment faced by Black nurses in The Netherlands is often subtle and of an "everyday" nature. For instance, she writes that they are often accused of theft, considered "stupid" when they do not understand a Dutch dialect, stereotyped as being "irresponsible" and not allowed to speak Surinamese[15] in the workplace.

In her study, Essed[16] discusses the fear White nurses have of Black solidarity. The maintenance of a "temporary" and "migrant" pool of Caribbean nursing assistants in Canada in the early 1950s was also a way of ensuring a lack of solidarity and thus vulnerability of these workers.

*Research Methodology* Since 1993, I have become aware of a number of cases of human rights violations of Black nurses in their workplaces. In some of them, I served as an expert witness. I have looked in-depth at some of these alleged human rights violations by reviewing various reports of the Ontario Human Rights Commission (OHRC). I have also found a report by Doris Marshall Institute (DMI) and Arnold Minors and Associates[17] very useful in understanding workplace racism. The two latter organizations were contracted by a hospital in Toronto in 1993 to help develop management and employment strategies to promote and ensure ethno-racial equality in the hospital. Beginning in 1990, seven Black nurses and one Filipino nurse from the hospital had filed complaints with the Ontario Human Rights Commission for being subjected to racial harassment and in some cases being fired or forced to resign. After a period of four years, the nurses won their cases, and a settlement was reached with the hospital.

The consultants hired by the hospital held a number of group interviews, one with the board and one with senior and middle managers. Other interviews were individually conducted. The consultants noted that the interviews were not completely successful:

"Staff are very reluctant to talk, and take extreme precaution when giving information; have fear of reprisals...."[18]

The consultants also reviewed the hospital's management manual, its newsletters from September 1992 to September 1993, its philosophy statement, minutes from a variety of meetings in which the hospital was involved, raw data from a survey conducted internally which drew 357 returns, OHRC reports and other related documents.

I have also undertaken an interview with a staff member of Ontario Nurses Association (ONA)[19] to develop a more global view of the problem. Finally, I attended a conference[20] in Toronto, which brought together Black registered nurses and other healthcare workers. In the course of this conference, I heard five healthcare professionals, including four registered nurses, present stories of racial harassment at their hospitals. One of the main purposes of sharing these stories was to establish links and support each other. Following the conference, a meeting was called to plan and organize a Black Nurses and Other Healthcare Workers Association.

In addition, I have relied on an article by Stan Gray[21] referred to earlier where he documents the experience of a senior Black woman who worked as a nurse's aide at a Toronto hospital and who was forced into early retirement. The woman contends that she was subjected to age and racial discrimination.

Overall, I am relying on the personal experiences of ten Black healthcare professionals, nine of them registered nurses in Ontario, apart from the secondary sources that I have already acknowledged. In addition, I draw on an interview with a key informant, a staff person from the Ontario Nurses' Association (ONA). Owing to ethical considerations, I have used fictitious names to identify nurses and hospitals, apart from the ones who are named already in secondary sources. All the hospitals I examined are large in size, based in metropolitan areas in Ontario and have multi-racial or multi-ethnic workforces, but managed overwhelmingly by White personnel.

## The Big Picture: Political Economy of Healthcare

As reported by Armstrong et al,[22] the current phase of healthcare policy is marked by cost-cutting through such means as restructuring, privatization and de-institutionalization. This has had profound and mostly negative effects on the nursing profession and on patient care. For instance, in the name of "quality assurance", nurses are now being monitored more through "form filling." Campbell[23] has also discussed this development. Changes in hospital work schedules include laying off full-time nurses while increasing those on part-time shifts and "floating" nurses and volunteers. These changes, all in the name of "employee empowerment," have seriously reduced the continuity and quality of patient care, and adversely affected the "team spirit" so crucial in this profession. Simultaneously, there has been a rise in staff conflicts; there is more management and hierarchy, nurses are being asked to "report on" each other, there is more disciplinary action against nurses, and more harassment in general. Restructuring is being undertaken in hospitals too fast, in the absence of proper training of both staff nurses and nurse managers. Moreover, scientific management principles are being introduced in hospitals without any thought to the impact on patient care, let alone on employees. Wotherspoon[24] discusses the fact that nurses are caught in two contradictory dynamics: 1) their demands for professionalization and a return to community-based healthcare; and, 2) proletarianization and gender subordination. Even though hospitals are arguing that the current economic crises in healthcare has not had any significant negative effect on care,[25] nurses and other healthcare employees insist that "quality care has gone out the window."[26] Some hospitals have implemented American models of healthcare based on the concepts of a low-paid, deskilled and non-unionized staff.[27] National surveys of nurses in Canada reveal dissatisfaction over staff shortages, workload, and quality of patient care.[28]

Restructuring in healthcare has also reduced the importance of "emotional labour" in nursing.[29] The latter is commonly referred to as "bedside manner" and refers to "working through frightening or worrying feelings and helping ill people and their families...work out a strategy they can live with." This work of emotional management requires skills particular to women congruent to gender ideology. Given the nature of patriarchy, emotional labour and its associated skills are not particularly valued in our society and it is even more devalued under fiscal "crisis." Ironically, it is emotional labour that is most "appreciated", not necessarily "valued", by patients and their families.

Most of the studies on healthcare crises and its effects on patient care and on labour relations have the limitation of being race-blind. It is assumed that the impact of reorganization and increased surveillance of nurses is uniform to *all* nurses. My research reveals that Black nurses, other nurses of colour and in a few instances militant White nurses are being adversely affected and experiencing it in different ways. Stan Gray[30] confirms this in a recent article where he documents the experience of a Black woman who worked as a nurse's aide in a Toronto hospital. She was subjected to harassment, suspended from work for alleged patient abuse and finally forced into early retirement. She believes that her harassment happened because of the "downsizing of healthcare."

The literature is also class-blind in most instances. Nursing managers are generally registered nurses (RNs) as are staff nurses. However, most nurses of colour work as staff nurses, and are the most adversely affected by fiscal constraints and management strategies. White nursing managers are key players in the daily harassment of these nurses. Therefore, by generalizing the impact on *all* nurses, one is also obfuscating class differences among different categories of RNs.

## Racism in the Wards

Following are more specific examples of how racism is experienced by mainly African-Canadian nurses on a daily basis. Similar experiences by other women of colour, such as Chinese-Canadian nurses, are also referred to.

Targeting outspoken nurses of colour seems to be a common experience. Typically, a Black nurse is singled out and subjected to differential treatment by management compared to White workers. This often takes the form of negative documentation being obtained from direct supervisors and colleagues on nurses of colour and accumulating this to be used later for discipline. One nurse said:

"Black nurses are reprimanded for coming late for break-times. All nurses are committing errors, but only nurses of colour are documented and reprimanded...."[31]

One healthcare worker[32] said that she had been labelled as "incompetent", even though there was no formal complaint filed and her work "performance was great." One nurse argued that she knows of instances where documentation was fabricated in order to "frame" nurses of colour. The following is her description of how this can happen:

"... camps form on the unit and then war is on ... feel very nervous ... very intimidated, being watched, documented ... they ask the opposition camp to document and they will fabricate...."[33]

Gray[34] writes of a 61-year-old Black nurse's aide who was allegedly "framed" twice with patient abuse because she was targeted by hospital management for early retirement. When she refused the retirement offer, she was subjected to harassment and charged with patient abuse, along with another senior registered practical nurse who also happens to be Black. That charge was dropped because of "lack of merit." In the second charge, a patient's sitter complained about her. Management immediately suspended her from work, despite a discipline-free work record spanning 26 years. The following describes what happened when she returned to work:

> "Cynthia was told she was no longer qualified to be a nurse's aide. She was immediately shunted to cleaning toilets, beds and floors...."[35]

The alleged incompetencies of these nurses are not dealt with in the same manner as most white nurses. A staff member from ONA said:

> "White nurses who've made mistakes have been helped and improved, whereas Black nurses are being set up to fail.... In remedial programs they are being followed very closely...."[36]

She continues:

> "People are disciplined differently and treated differently...."

The DMI report confirms this perspective. It notes:

> Disciplinary measures are lenient towards White staff; swift and unbending towards people of colour. For example, tardiness by a white person is ignored, even if it is a frequent occurrence; racial minority staff are immediately warned, even put under surveillance, for tardiness. One was dismissed due to tardiness which was her first offence in three years of employment.[37]

The accusation of incompetency of Black nurses, fabricated or not, immediately leads to summary dismissals or suspensions of the targeted nurses. One nurse[38] was fired within a few days of being first made aware that her performance was lacking, thus violating the policy of progressive discipline in her hospital. She was penalized for deficiencies for which White nurses are seldom disciplined, and rarely dismissed.

Another nurse[39] tells of being suspended from work without pay after an argument with a White colleague. In addition, she was not to be assigned any leadership role for a period of time. On the other hand, the white nurse was not disciplined and was assigned a leadership position, even though she was junior to the Black nurse.

Another nurse said that she was dismissed on grounds of making "several" medication errors. Some minor errors may have been made, but she was, in fact, accused of making many more than were entailed.

"… the client's well-being is primary … the College of Nurses says that we should start with systemic problems rather than individual problems. This is not followed in most cases. It mostly leads to disciplinary action…."[40]

Scapegoating is a common experience when Black nurses and other nurses of colour are subjected to false accusations, blaming and disciplining for unwanted events or actions in which they were not the sole participants. Nurses of colour are often blamed for conflicts with patients, other colleagues and for faulty nursing practices, e.g. incorrect medication delivery. In situations of staff conflict, scapegoated nurses are often taken to task even though they may actually have been the victims of harassment. In one case, a nurse[41] was given a counselling letter following a patient's complaint letter about her. The latter was subsequently placed in the nurse's file even though the patient's family members had been aggressive towards her to the point of being "physical". She was penalized for the incident and the fact that she had been physically threatened was not mentioned or dealt with anywhere.

Another nurse[42] delivered a baby who died minutes after birth. She reported that she was questioned by hospital officials for months after the event, even though the mother and other family members were completely satisfied with her efforts. She was transferred to another unit and subjected to other forms of harassment.

Excessive monitoring can be a way in which a Black nurse is targeted so that s/he feels constantly watched, judged and threatened with the prospect of being framed for dismissal. The crucial point in this process is that similar monitoring is not happening for white nurses. It contributes to a "poisoned" environment. An ONA staff member describes how this happens:

> "... They (Black) nurses are supervised closely ... you get so nervous ... afraid to make mistakes ... supervisor asks questions or comments to confuse ... not helpful or constructive ... there was one case of a nurse of colour who had to use a piece of equipment that White nurses don't have to do ... the union became involved and the supervisor backed off."[43]

One senior nurse[44] tells of her manager accompanying her and unnecessarily lecturing her on simple and ordinary procedures with patients. A file of negative documentation was also compiled against this nurse, subsequently leading to her termination.

Marginalization is a result of isolation. Isolation can happen for various reasons, but it is more likely to occur if a person of colour is working in a predominantly White environment, or if the employee lacks empathy from managers or co-workers. In cases of alleged racism experienced by Black nurses from White patients and their relatives, it is not unusual for management to deny the possibility of racism and to "lump" in racism with other negative behaviours from patients. It seems that management fails to recognize the differential impact on Black nurses of a patient who is angry because of a "care" issue and one who is angry and racist. The following excerpt from the DMI report is an example of marginalization:

> [The] patient said: "Get your Black hands off me." Or, without being asked, would say: "Yes, I'd like to have a White nurse." Unit managers would not back up staff, when they complain about this abusive language. The result is that patients continue to be abusive, knowing that such behaviour is being tolerated.[45]

Thus, racial incidents are not followed up and investigated. In fact, it is believed that racism does not exist. By denying the existence of racism, Black nurses are further marginalized and unsupported. In one case, a nurse[46] was issued a formal warning letter after a patient's relative complained about the quality of her patient care. The nurse alleges that the patient's relative had made a racist remark towards Black nurses. The latter allegation was not fully investigated by management, and was, in fact, dismissed.

In another case, a nurse[47] was physically threatened by a patient's relative for alleged neglect and he was heard to make a racist and sexist comment. Although management recognized the physical safety issue brought up by this incident, it did not acknowledge nor address the aggressive racism that was expressed against the nurse.

Solidarity among Black nurses is often seen as a threat by White management. This is ironic since management often systemically segregates Black nurses so that they work in similar floors and departments. The perceived threat of Black nurses' solidarity is sometimes dealt with by management by dispersing and separating them, for example by assigning them different break times, or by strongly discouraging their association through threats and intimidation. The following are some testimonies:

"… one nurse of colour will not back up other nurses of colour for fear of retaliation…."[48]

"… I became afraid of repercussion on friend … fear for self and family … endangering my license, my life, anyone who's close to me…."[49]

"… I was transferred to another unit to separate me from my colleagues in the unit who would have supported me…."[50]

Infantalization of Black nurses is also prevalent when they are subjected to condescension, belittling, "put downs", and labelled as "not being good enough." For instance, the ONA representative interviewed said there was a general "lack of tolerance" towards nurses for whom English is a second language or a second dialect. They are accused of not having communication skills and of "asking too many questions" if they attempt to clarify terminology with which they may be unfamiliar.[51] Almost every nurse who spoke at the *End the Silence* conference mentioned they had been characterized as having "a communication problem." One nurse related the following case involving a Chinese-Canadian:

"... she was removed from the operating room to do clerical work, housekeeping work, 'Joe' jobs...."[52]

The DMI report cites the following testimony:

It was found that Black nurses were censured for speaking in local dialects among themselves, Italian and Portuguese nurses, for example, were freely allowed to speak their first languages to one another.[53]

Black nurses are often unnecessarily criticized for the quality of work. Sometimes they are patronizingly directed to take courses which are far below their actual skills or experienced Black nurses with years of seniority will be lectured unnecessarily on a simple procedure. One nurse[54] who was subjected to racism and to aggressive behaviour by a patient's relatives was referred to a workshop on crisis intervention. This action trivialized the traumatic impact of racial harassment on her, and implied that she was to blame for the handling of the incident.

Blaming the victim is a related practice in these hospitals; management will often blame Black nurses for the nurses' misfortunes, including their experiences of racism. Nurses[55] who have complained about racism have been accused of "using" racism to divert attention from their own deficiencies, thus denying their experience completely. It is implied that these nurses are dishonest, unreliable and have a "chip on their shoulder." The DMI report quotes management's position with regard to the complaints made to the Ontario Human Rights Commission by Black nurses and nurses of colour on account of racial discrimination:

In the hospital's press release of March 27, 1991, I indicated that dismissals and disciplinary actions against employees are based on their behaviour and compliance with standards of practice, and are not racially motivated. This remains the hospital's position....[56]

Bias in work allocation and a segregated workforce is evident in hospitals, where Black nurses and other nurses of colour are assigned to heavier duties in less specialized areas, given less desirable shifts and units, knowing that some of these nurses have considerable experience and skills and some have physical disabilities that are not accomodated. This fact was reiterated by several nurses at the "End the Silence" conference. One nurse[57] also mentioned that nurses of colour are often assigned patients of colour. The DMI report mentions that nurses of colour are commonly streamed into chronic care and away from acute care, such as surgery.[58]

The ONA informant confirmed that there is evidence of over-representation of nurses of colour in "heavier" units which are not considered the pinnacle of nursing. For instance, in a number of large hospitals, 70 per cent of the nurses in the veterans' wing and in the long-term care unit are nurses of colour.[59] She further cited a case where a director of nursing in such an unit issued a memo to nurses just prior to the Caribana[60] weekend saying "if you call in sick this weekend, you have to bring in a doctor's note." This was obviously directed at Black nurses and the ONA was able to challenge this successfully.

In general, Black nurses are also treated differentially and adversely with regard to "good shifts", lunch breaks and vacations.[61]

Most nurses in leadership positions, e.g., head nurses, team leaders and charge nurses, are White and hospitals are overwhelmingly run by White management. An ONA staff person confirmed that there are few Black nurse managers. She estimated that in Ontario there are less than five Black or Filipinos in senior managerial positions, with more of them being Filipino than Black.[62] Often, a junior white nurse will be trained to take on a leadership role while a senior black nurse will be passed over.

Underemployment and the denial of promotions are also evident among Black nurses in hospitals. They are often discouraged from applying for leadership positions on the basis of "lack of skills" or lack of competence. Several nurses at the *End the Silence* conference spoke about having trained White nurses who subsequently became managers. They also spoke about Black women "not being approached" to be managers. An internal hospital report states:

It was felt that the chances of advancement and promotion within the hospital are very limited, particularly with respect to Black nurses. Apparently there are no Black managers. Considering the percentage of staff which is Black, this was felt to be unfair and very bad for staff morale.[63]

Many Black nurses find their supervisors are disbelieving and unaccommodating when they complain of a particular disability or illness. These nurses are often asked to bring doctor's notes and medical clearance to prove themselves whereas White nurses are not asked to do the same. In one case, a Black nurse,[64] still recovering from an illness, refused to work at night because she felt she was still not well enough to work that shift given that there is less staffing support. The management concluded that she was lying and she was subsequently fired, partly as result of this incident.

One nurse at the *End the Silence* conference mentioned the following incident:

> "One nurse [of colour] was sick and went home. [The] manager stated that she had "abandoned" her patients and was going to be reported to the college."[65]

Whether or not this nurse had a replacement to take over her shift makes no difference as far as management reactions are concerned. In all the cases of which I am aware, nurses were still disciplined by management, even though a replacement was found in every case.

Co-optation of individual nurses of colour and selective alliances with nursing staff are sometimes used in order to monitor outspoken Black nurses targeted by management for disciplinary action. As mentioned earlier, co-opted nurses may collude in the fabrication of documentation in order to "frame" an outspoken nurse of colour. Some of the testimonies reported in the DMI report address this issue directly:

> "Some nurses were requested by their nurse managers to spy on their co-workers and to report back with information which could later be used against those employees."[66]

> "I fell ill because of harassment I received at the hands of my manager. My blood pressure went up, and I was in severe shock; I was intimidated, berated, yelled at and threatened due to my refusal to bear false witness against my supervisor, a woman of colour. When I refused to co-operate, I was told my behaviour is insubordinate...."[67]

When accused of racism, management in hospitals and other institutions will point to "token" managers of colour in order to prove their commitment to equality of opportunity. What is downplayed is the fact that management is overwhelmingly White and people of colour are rare exceptions.

### Contextualizing Everyday Racism in Hospitals

In the preceding section, I described some of the most common experiences of racism faced by Black nurses in hospitals. These experiences tell us about White management practices and also about the way employment systems operate in these hospitals. Management practices may be standard or differential, conscious or unconscious, but all have an adverse effect on most Black nurses and other nurses of colour. This is systemic racism in the workplace. In other words, individual practices by managers are based on racism evident in the employment systems of these hospitals, including the everyday culture of the workplace. In the next section, I will link management practices with racist employment systems.

As mentioned, leadership in these hospitals is predominantly White. This is a result of subjective promotional procedures. For example, a nursing unit manager, usually White, often will "name" who will fill a particular leadership position. Pre-screening, checking of references, interviews and internal transfers are often left to one person, usually a White female manager. This reliance on one person making choices leaves room for subjectivity and biases which creep into the decision-making structure. For instance, it was reported by Hardill[68] that:

During hiring, one reference check was generally completed for White nurses; three references were commonly checked before hiring Black nurses... Personnel files and job application forms for black nurses frequently contained personal and irrelevant information about their families, place of origin and English proficiency.[69]

It is also evident that the selection of nurses for leadership positions is inconsistent. For instance, in one unit, a team leader's position may be rotated; in another unit, nurses with special training may be preferred for these positions. This shows that *ad hoc* methods are used to fill leadership positions based on the style of individual managers. This affects Black nurses adversely, as evident from their testimonies.

Some of these hospitals use word-of-mouth recruitment methods. Various reports on employment equity have pointed out that word-of-mouth recruitment can act as a barrier to the employment of people of colour and women in non-traditional jobs and sectors. It basically reproduces the status quo. Therefore, if the labour force in an establishment is racially segmented and predominantly female, then the word-of-mouth approach will merely reproduce that pattern.

In some hospitals, internal candidates are given first preference at times and, at other times, the competition is opened to those in the external labour market. The inconsistency in the outreach process is a concern from an employment equity perspective. Who decides when the competition will be open and when it will be closed? Biases are sure to operate, as such important decisions are often left to one or two management staff.

When job interviews are being conducted by individual managers, it is imperative that training be given in employment equity measures. As there is an overwhelming denial of racism by hospital management, such an approach is not likely to be adopted. It is evident that interviewers often use vague, subjective criteria to select personnel. The suitability of candidates is often judged by the external presentation of the candidate in the interview situation. It is apparent that candidates may be judged on verbal fluency and non-verbal cues, most likely based on cultural, class and gender biases. Effective styles of communication tend to be associated with the styles of people who are already in the organization[70] therefore those who present themselves "differently" may be viewed as "less effective." An interviewer who is unfamiliar with cross-cultural issues, such as the ones in these hospitals, can assign negative values to candidates' verbal and non-verbal cues and thus judge their suitability for a job in a biased and an incorrect way.

Similar biases seem to flourish within the employee appraisal systems, where vague and subjective criteria are often used to judge people's job performance. For instance, several nurses reported being judged negatively on "communication skills" or on "personality problems." Frequently, no further specifications are provided on these criteria so that the supervisor conducting the appraisal can interpret these terms in her own way. In other words, vague criteria provide the scope for arbitrary decisions influenced by one's prejudices and power position. Also, employee appraisals are used to determine if an employee should be promoted or granted a permanent position.

It appears that disciplinary measures are also taken in non-standard ways and are therefore prone to supervisory biases. In light of the biases evident in the outreach, recruitment and appraisal processes, suspensions and firings of Black nurses and other nurses of colour need to be questioned. There are several examples of differential disciplinary measures being taken with Black and White nurses. Also, the apparent failure to deal with performance concerns of some Black nurses in a constructive manner that is directed to improvement indicates inconsistent disciplinary procedures.

The handling of medication errors in hospitals creates concerns from an employment equity perspective. It is not surprising that many Black nurses have reported they have been unfairly accused of making "too many medication errors," and disciplined, as a result, in some cases actually being dismissed from their jobs. The purpose of documenting medication errors is not consistently and clearly understood by management and nursing staff in hospitals. Some believe it is there to discipline nurses, or used to periodically review the medication delivery system. Others believe it serves as a safeguard against lawsuits. The policy surrounding this issue seems to be cut and dry, but, in practice a great deal of discretion remains at every level. On what basis are these discretionary decisions taken? Is it based on any set guidelines, or is it subjective? When most head nurses are White, there is cause for concern if the alleged error has been made by a Black nurse.

By and large, these hospitals do not have practical anti-harassment policies and complaints procedures, particularly where it concerns racial harassment. Where a policy exists, it may be unknown to employees and clients, and specific guidelines to deal with racist incidents will be lacking.

The everyday experiences of racism described here, become logical if seen in the context of systemic racism and sexism in the employment systems of hospitals. Scapegoating, targeting and excessive monitoring by management are not surprising given the biases built into the employee performance appraisal and in the disciplinary measures taken. In both of these management functions, the use of vague, subjective, and non-stand-ardized criteria results in differential treatment of Black and White nurses.

The marginalization of Black female workers in a predominantly White female workforce is predictable, given the racial segregation which exists. Biased recruitment, outreach and interview processes lead to a racially segregated workforce. Also, a predominantly White manage-ment with no training in cross-cultural, anti-racist and anti-sexist issues, and lacking a viable policy on racial harassment, will be ill-equipped to respond to and deal effectively with racist incidents.

Underemployment and the lack of promotions among Black nurses are natural consequences of work environments in which there are no stand-ard and objective procedures for employee performance appraisals.

Co-optation, selective alliances and tokenism have to be viewed in the context of the nature of hospital leadership. As mentioned, the latter is predominantly White, lacking in cross-cultural and anti-racist skills, per-ceiving Black female workers in stereotypical ways, including feeling threatened by them, and not guided by any policy on racial harassment. The traditional management method of divide and rule is the only one they know, and that is what is often used.

Management actions *vis à vis* Black nurses also betray its entrenched system of stereotypes and prejudices, most of which arose out of slavery and have now become part of the everyday culture of racism. This culture of racism is evident in the culture of hospitals. Stereotypes about Black people as being "childlike", "inferior", "unskilled" and "dishonest," un-derlie the practices of infantalization, blaming the victim, bias in work al-location, underemployment and lack of accommodation for their disabili-ties. The following testimonies from White staff members documented by DMI and Minors illustrate common stereotypes and prejudices held about Black nurses:

"Some Black employees are very slow. If they were White, they wouldn't last."

"Nurses trained in Jamaica come with below average standards and need extra training."

"There are some people who don't feel as committed or as integrated; for example, some people from the islands...."

"When it came to the work ethic, people in Nigeria didn't grow up with nose to the grindstone; they wanted to be laid back and have fun. But if they come here where we are more disciplined, problems occur because some people here do not understand cultural differences...."

"I feel that visible minorities are excessively sensitive and do not take responsibility for their actions. Their lack of self confidence leads them to accuse everyone else, and lay the blame elsewhere. There is no evidence of racism in the hospital."[71]

The daily harassment of Black nurses and other health professionals give us a glimpse of what can happen in a racist, sexist culture where Black women workers with high levels of skill and leadership qualities challenge the status quo. Individuals who have much to gain from the status quo, i.e., those with relative power, White in most instances, struggle to put Black women back in their "ascribed" place. In discussing the sexual harassment of "X", a Black woman worker in a predominantly male, White workforce, Bannerji[72] writes:

The expectations from X obviously were that she should fit some common notion of her "natural" inferiority as a black woman and should also "know her place"....

Bannerji further describes this form of harassment as a "racist sexual harassment". A similar dynamic is apparent in the case of Black nurses in hospitals, except that they are working in predominantly female workforces. The form of harassment is definitely a "classist racial harassment," one in which employees are disciplined and punished by "superiors" for being in the wrong place in terms of class and racially-prescribed roles, and for challenging the stereotypes of "what Black people should be like".

In addition, it is also apparent that these nurses are also challenging the stereotypes of where Black women "should be" within the workplace.

Being registered nurses, with seniority, playing leadership roles with junior nurses (frequently White), other nursing personnel and patients (of diverse racial and ethnic backgrounds), these Black women are violating gender norms, which are laced with racism and class ideologies. Interestingly, White female managers often characterize Black nurses in the same way White males have done since the days of slavery. Black nurses are frequently described as "yelling and screaming", "threatening", reducing white colleagues "to tears", intimidating, dangerous, insensitive, and "cruel". Stereotypes about Black women being "troublemakers" and "evil" underlie White, female management paranoia about Black solidarity and the targeting of outspoken nurses. The denial of Black women's experiences of racism, illness and disability by White female managers seems to reproduce assumptions about the former's "toughness" and "Amazon quality", almost to the point of being non-human. With such characterizations, Black female nurses are portrayed as the antithesis of the "feminine", a reversal of the soft-spoken or silent, acquiescing, nurturing, serving, compassionate and kind female figure associated with "White femininity" and with the nursing profession. White female nursing managers who are responsible for evaluating staff nurses, and who have used their privilege to document racist, sexist impressions are in effect saying that Black women should not be in this profession because they are "not qualified". By these characterizations, Black women are being "nullified as women" and therefore rendered unskilled in terms which have traditionally defined this profession as "women's work". "They" are considered unqualified because of the assumed deficiency in their nursing skills but also because of their personalities which are extensions of who they are – Black women!

## Notes

1. Pat and Hugh Armstrong, *Take Care: Warning Signals for Canada's Health System*, (Toronto: Garamond Press, 1994); Pat Armstrong, et al. *Vital Signs: Nursing in Transition*, (Toronto: Garamond Press, 1993); Marie Campbell, "Management as "Ruling": A Class Phenomenon in Nursing," *Studies in Political Economy*, 27 (Autumn, 1988).
2. Agnes Calliste, "Women of 'Exceptional Merit': Immigration of Caribbean Nurses to Canada," *Canadian Journal of Women and the Law*, Vol. 6, No.1, 1993, p. 95.
3. Wilson Head, *An Exploratory Study of Attitudes and Perceptions of Minority and Majority Group Healthcare Workers*, (Ontario: Ontario Ministry of Labour, 1985)

4. Philomena Essed, *Everyday Racism: Reports From Women of Two Cultures*, (California: Hunter House Inc., 1990)

5. Marina Lee-Cunin, *Daughters of Seacole: A Study of Black Nurses in West Yorkshire*, (West Yorkshire: West Yorkshire Low Pay Unit Ltd., 1989)

6. Agnes Calliste, "Women of 'Exceptional Merit': Immigration of Caribbean Nurses to Canada," *Canadian Journal of Women and the Law*, Vol. 6, No. 1, 1993, pp.85-102.

7. Calliste, "Exceptional Merit," p. 95.

8. Marina Lee-Cunin, *Daughters of Seacole: A Study of Black Nurses in West Yorkshire*, (West Yorkshire: West Yorkshire Low Pay Unit Ltd., 1989)

9. Calliste, "Exceptional Merit," p.100.

10. Head, *Exploratory Study*.

11. Head, *Exploratory Study*, p. 59.

12. Head, *Exploratory Study*.

13. Philomena Essed, *Everyday Racism: Report of Women of Two Cultures*, (California: Hunter House Inc., 1990)

14. Essed, *Everyday Racism*.

15. Surinam was a Dutch colony for about 400 years. Over 200,000 Surinamese people migrated to the Netherlands in the 1970s and 1980s.

16. Essed, *Everyday Racism*.

17. Doris Marshall Institute and Arnold Minors & Associates, *Ethno-Racial Equality: A Distant Goal? An Interim Report To Northwestern General Hospital*, Toronto, December 1993-January 1994.

18. DMI and Minors, *Ethno-Racial Equality*, p.34.

19. Valerie MacDonald, Coordinator, Employment Relations Service, ONA, interviewed by phone on October 13, 1993.

20. "End the Silence on Racism in the Health Care Field," A Conference for Black Nurses and Other Health Care Workers, Congress of Black Women of Canada Toronto Chapter, Ontario Institute of Studies in Education, May 26, 1995.

21. Stan Gray, "Hospitals and Human Rights,"*Our Times*, Vol. 13, No.6, December 1994, p.17-20.

22. Armstrong et al, *Take Care*, p. 53.

23. Campbell, "Management as Ruling".

24. Terry Wotherspoon, "The Impact of Healthcare De-Institutionalization on the Organization and Delivery of Nursing Services," in *Women, Medicine and Health* edited by B. Singh Bolaria and Rosemary Bolaria, (Halifax: Fernwood Publishing, 1994).

25. Lisa Priest, "Hospitals Helping More, Group Says," *The Toronto Star*, May 18, 1995, p. A34; Daniel Tatroff, "Under the Knife in Chilliwack," *Our Times*, Vol. 14, No.2, May/June 1995.

26. Geoff Meggs, "Quality Caring," *Our Times*, Vol. 14, No. 2, May/June 1995, p. 43.

27. For a case study of the effects of an American model being implemented in a B.C. hospital, see Tatroff, "Under the Knife in Chilliwack."

28. Discussed in Wotherspoon, "Impact of Healthcare," p. 265.

29. Byrad Yyelland, "Structural Constraints, Emotional Labour and Nursing Work," in B. Singh Bolaria and Rosemary Bolaria (eds.), *Women, Medicine and Health*, (Halifax: Fernwood Publishing, 1994), pp.231-240.

30. Stan Gray, "Hospitals and Human Rights", *Our Times*, Vol. 13, No. 6 (December, 1994), pp.17-20.

31. Debbie, "End the Silence" Conference, Toronto, May 26, 1995.

32. Terry, "End the Silence," May 26, 1995.

33. Debbie, "End the Silence," May 26, 1995.

34. Gray, "Hospitals," p.17.

35. Gray, "Hospitals," p. 17.

36. Telephone interview with Valerie MacDonald, Coordinator Employment Relations Services, ONA, October 13, 1993.

37. DMI and Minors, *Report*, p. 39.

38. Joan, OHRC documents.

39. Tracy, OHRC Complaint.

40. Mary, "End the Silence," May 26, 1995.

41. Tracy, OHRC Reports.

42. Wilma, "End the Silence," May 26, 1995.

43. MacDonald, October 13, 1993.

44. Joan, OHRC documents.

45. DMI and Minors, *Report*, p. 33.

46. Tracy, OHRC Reports.

47. Denise, OHRC Reports.

48. Debbie, "End the Silence", May 26, 1995.

49. Rosa, "End the Silence," May 26, 1995.

50. Wilma, "End the Silence," May 26, 1995.

51. MacDonald, October 13, 1993.

52. Debbie, "End the Silence," May 26, 1995.

53. DMI and Minors, *Ethno-Racial*, p. 35.

54. Tracy, OHRC documents.

55. Tracy. OHRC documents.

56. DMI and Minors, *Report*, p. 32.

57. Debbie, "End the Silence" conference, May 26, 1995.

58. DMI and Minors, *Ethno-Racial*, p.34.

59. MacDonald, October 13, 1993.

60. An annual weekend of celebration held each summer, organized by the Caribbean-Canadian community in Toronto.

61. DMI and Minors, *Ethno-Racial*, p. 37.

62. MacDonald, October 13, 1993.

63. DMI and Minors, *Ethno-Racial*, p. 35.

64. Marilyn, OHRC Reports.

65. Debbie, "End the Silence", May 26, 1995.

66. DMI and Minors, *Ethno-Racial Equality*, p. 35.

67. DMI and Minors, *Ethno-Racial*, p. 35.

68. Kathy Hardill, *Discovering Fire Where the Smoke Is: Racism in the Healthcare System, Towards Justice in Health,* Summer, 1993.

69. Quoted in DMI and Minors, *Ethno-Racial,* p.37.

70. City of Toronto, *Equal Opportunity: Detecting Bias: Part One,* (Toronto: City of Toronto, August 1983)p.40.

71. All the preceding quotes are from DMI and Minors, *Ethno-Racial,* p. 40-41.

72. Himani Bannerji, *Thinking Through: Essays on Feminism, Marxism, and Anti-Racism,* (Toronto: Women's Press, 1995), p. 142.

**Chapter 5**

# Resisting Racism
# in the Workplace

N O DISCUSSION of racism, sexism and classism is complete without ex
ploring the ways to resist or fight these oppressions. This chapter
will present a few options individuals and groups have used. These strategies combine aspects of advocacy, counselling, community education and
community action. They are not mutually exclusive and, in most situations, it is advisable to use more than one strategy.

## Unions

One of the best and quickest ways of redressing a case of racial harassment is to rely on anti-harassment and anti-discrimination clauses in
one's collective agreement. One advantage is that the grievance procedure that is prescribed is clear and time-specific so that the process is
relatively short and predictable. Moreover, the shop steward or other union official working on the case acts as an advocate of the griever and the
process is free of charge. However, it becomes more complicated if the
grievance is against another union member, i.e., if the alleged harasser is a
colleague. Unions have a variety of strategies to deal with such situations.[1] Some unions will not defend an offender. Others prefer to only
grieve against management since the latter is obliged to provide a work
environment free of harassment. If a co-worker is harassing someone,
management should intervene and end the harassment. If the harasser is
being harassed in turn by management, then the union will grieve on the
employee's behalf. Even though the union grievance procedure is one of
the most expedient ways of fighting racism, sexism and some forms of
classism, its strength largely depends on the union membership, the commitment of union officials to human rights issues, the internal education

of union members and the allocation of resources directed to anti-harassment cases. Some grievers have had the unfortunate experience of not being assisted by their shop stewards because they did not think there was a "solid case." In addition, if a worker is non-unionized or belongs to a union which does not have anti-discrimination and anti-harassment clauses in its collective agreement, or if these concepts are not clearly defined and understood, then that worker will not be able to grieve on the basis of harassment. Approximately 41 per cent[2] of workers in Canada are unionized and many people of colour and immigrant workers are in sectors that are non-unionized, such as homework or in subcontracted work. Even if a worker is unionized and has anti-harassment and anti-discrimination clauses in her contract, she may feel intimidated in bringing forward a grievance because of the very real fear of being subjected to further harassment, or even dismissal. A worker with a basic level of English may be unable to read and understand the legal language of most collective agreements, and, in the absence of translations and internal educational sessions by unions, the worker may even be unaware of the agreement's anti-discrimination clauses.

The Ontario Federation of Labour (OFL) launched the "Racism Hurts Everyone" campaign in 1981 with a coordinator, hired under a one-year contract. Since that time, there have been many ups and downs in the campaign and many internal struggles, some of which have been documented.[3] The Ontario Coalition of Black Trade Unionists (OCBTU), developed in 1986 and led by Black unionists and unionists of colour, demanded stronger human rights clauses in contracts and the implementation of employment equity within the OFL itself.

The OFL's efforts have concentrated on the drafting of the Employment Equity Regulations in Ontario. Unions were to have played a significant role in the implementation of employment equity, e.g., in areas of joint responsibility with employers. Most activities dealt with training staff representatives and building leadership within unions to undertake this responsibility. After the Progressive Conservative election victory in 1995, Ontario Premier Mike Harris, who ran his campaign on an anti-equity platform, moved quickly to dismantle the Employment Equity Commission based in Toronto and eliminate the Employment Equity Act and its regulations.

## Human Rights Commissions

All provinces in Canada have human rights commissions and are covered by human rights codes which prohibit discrimination on the basis of race, sex and colour.

The prohibited grounds of discrimination can be waived if the employer can prove that discrimination is a "bona fide occupational requirement"[4] and that the cost of accommodating a person from a prohibited category is "undue hardship ... considering the cost, outside sources of funding, if any, and health and safety requirements, if any."[5] For instance, "a religious, philanthropic, educational, fraternal or social institution or organization" which primarily serves a particular community defined by religion, race, sex, ethnic origin or other prohibited grounds for discrimination, can give preference in employment to someone from its own community, thereby discriminating against someone who is not. Also, an individual who wants to hire someone to care for an ill child or other relative can discriminate on prohibited grounds.

The provincial human rights commissions have prescribed processes for dealing with complaints of discrimination, which includes the filing of the complaint by the griever, the investigation of the complaint by a commission officer, the conciliation and then either its dismissal or recommended transfer to a board of inquiry. Only a minority of cases are sent to the board for further investigation, after which they are dismissed. If the griever is still unsatisfied with the results then she/he can pursue a civil suit in Divisional Court, Court of Appeal or to the Supreme Court of Canada.

The Ontario Human Rights Commission has come under severe criticism by community groups and advocates on human rights issues. Some of their main complaints have been that the process is too long due to a backlog of cases and lack of resources, that human rights officers see themselves as neutral individuals in situations where the griever is clearly in a more vulnerable and powerless situation, and that the procedure of dealing with complaints definitely gives an upper-hand to the perpetrator, especially if the perpetrator is an employer. Furthermore, many feel there is no enforcement of the code, and the process further victimizes the griever.[6] In one instance, a griever had to wait for six years until a board of inquiry was set up to hear her case.[7] Gray writes that a Task Force set up by the provincial government to investigate the OHRC confirmed these concerns, and further revealed that members of groups that are regularly discriminated against have lost all confidence in the commission. Another criticism of the provincial commissions has been that they have an individual, case-by-case approach, which does not address situations of systemic discrimination in employment. A much awaited "systemic investigations unit" set up by the OHRC was disbanded recently after investigating one landmark case which involved seven Black nurses and one Filipino nurse from Northwestern General Hospital in Toronto. On the basis of these inadequacies described above, some have called for the dismantling of the OHRC and the redeployment of resources into aiding complainants who file civil suits.[8]

A number of reports[9] have also highlighted racism within the OHRC itself, particularly as it is experienced by workers of colour. Tokenism, harassment of Black officers, racial segmentation, differential training opportunities on the basis of colour, a climate of racism and systemic racism in hiring and promotions[10] were mentioned among other problems. Young[11] analyzed racism entrenched in the process of handling complaints against racism, for instance in common stereotypes, assumptions and prejudices that officers have about complainants of colour. These biased attitudes adversely deny justice and equal treatment to complainants largely by a process of trivialization and invalidation of statements.

Presumably, the Anti-racism Committee of the OHRC is working towards identifying and analyzing racism within the commission and also developing strategies of eliminating the problems identified. To my knowledge, no other provincial commission has initiated a similar self-analysis.

There is also a Canadian Human Rights Commission which prohibits discrimination on race, colour, national or ethnic origin, religion, sex, to name a few of the prohibitive grounds. It does not, however, prohibit discrimination on ancestry, nationality, citizenship, or creed. The difference between the federal and provincial commissions is a jurisdictional one, the CHRC covering cases outside provincial domain such as federal departments, crown corporations and chartered banks.

## Community Actions

Immigrant workers and people of colour, including women, have found it imperative to rely on resources within their own communities to get the necessary response from human rights commissions and business enterprises. This holds especially true when fighting cases of human rights violations in the workplace. In May, 1994, in a highly publicized case, (referred to earlier), concerning Black nurses at the Northwestern General Hospital, the eight grievers won a settlement with the perpetrators when the case had reached a Board of Inquiry of the OHRC. The settlement was mediated by Stephen Lewis,[12] who had been specially appointed by the provincial government. The case had continued for four years and it is clear that the nurses won because of the strong community support they received from groups such as the Congress of Black Women. They were also supported by the Ontario Nurses Association. In addition, the hospital had to commit itself to concrete measures of addressing systemic racism within its employment systems.

In October 1982, 23 South Asian women[13] who worked in a non-unionized Toronto factory in the same shift were unfairly fired for demanding a raise of 30 cents an hour which had been given to another shift which was predominantly Italian. The women filed complaints against their employer with the OHRC on the basis of racism. Soon after, a support committee made up of community workers, legal aid workers, some union activists and many individuals from the South Asian community, was formed. This committee undertook many actions of solidarity, such as public meetings, press releases, delegations, political lobbying, and so on. Within a short period of time, the labour minister appointed a mediator to resolve the case. By December of that year, the women workers were all reinstated in their jobs with the desired 30-cent-an-hour raise. The women would have had no hope of having their complaint even looked at by an investigating officer before the end of that year, had it been left to the OHRC. The case also revealed a loophole in the provincial Employment Standards Act which leaves non-unionized workers unprotected from unjust dismissals. The labour minister promised to look into it,[14] but the problem still exists today.

Of course, not every community action leads to such positive outcomes. Cases of racial harassment at work involving John Persaud[15] and Wei Fu[16] resulted in large, community-based support committees that engaged in tireless actions to expedite the cases. However, after lengthy processes, the two cases were dismissed by boards of inquiry, where the chairperson of both actions (incidentally the same person) chose to ignore racial slurs and other forms of harassment by superiors or at best described them as being "morally wrong" (in the case of Fu) and as being "exemplary" (in the case of Persaud).

## Community Organizations

A community initiative has been formed in Toronto called the Task Force for Anti-Racism Action Centre,[17] led by Women Working with Immigrant Women (WWIW) and the Cross Cultural Communication Centre (CCCC).[18] The task force membership, including a wide variety of community and labour organizations, is committed to establishing a centre which will provide one-to-one individual support, counselling, referrals, and follow-up to those who have experienced racism and who are seeking redress. It will also bring grievers into groups and link up organizations in the area engaged in anti-racism work. The need for such a centre was identified in a conference organized by WWIW in 1989 and also an earlier study that it conducted entitled "Racial Minority Women and Race Relations."

Once established, the community centre will be unique in providing emotional support to those who have human rights grievances.

## Employment Equity

Employment equity as a strategy to address workplace discrimination was first mentioned by Judge Rosalie Abella[19]. It is meant to be a program which identifies discrimination in employment, to redress that situation and to ensure that previously excluded groups are in fact represented within the workplace. The program[20] includes the preparation of the workforce in any establishment, including a management statement of commitment to the concept, a communication and educational strategy to help workers and management understand the concept of employment equity, the identification of discriminatory structures and barriers within the workplace, and finally to develop goals and timetables to hire and promote previously under-represented groups. The last step includes conducting a workforce analysis to compare representation of groups within the establishment with their availability in the larger population. The "target groups" are women, visible minorities (the term used by the Canadian Government to describe people of colour), Native Peoples and people with disabilities.

In 1986, the Employment Equity Act was brought into effect by the Federal Government. However, this legislation has been critiqued by many community groups because it is very limited in its scope, with no goals or timetables, no reviews and no enforcement. In effect, it is a voluntary program. The legislation covers federally owned or regulated crown corporations with more than 100 employees,but this excludes the federal government itself. It is obvious that the program is very limited particularly as it affects people of colour and immigrant workers, most of whom work in smaller establishments and in the government itself. The employers who are covered by the act are required to collect workforce data and then file it with the Canadian Human Rights Commission. Although there may be penalties for not fulfilling this requirement, there is no penalty for not developing an employment equity program.

The federal government also has a Contract Compliance Program in which any company bidding for a government contract of over $200,000 has to prove that they intend to develop an employment equity program. Upon review, if the company fails to prove this, then it can be fined up to $50,000 and lose the contract, but only after a number of warnings and with the approval of a minister.

Some equity advocates have argued that the federal employment equity program has not been successful because it has been "top-down" and not geared to "statistical improvement."[21] It seems that most of the federally-regulated employers are concentrating on removing biases from the outreach, screening and interview processes and concentrating less on actually increasing representation from the target groups.

In Ontario, the Employment Equity Act and its regulations came into operation on September 1, 1994. However, as mentioned, the Harris government is eliminating the Act and its regulations. The provincial Act was much broader than its federal counterpart because it covered workers in the private sector, and the broader public sector including municipalities, school boards, colleges, universities, hospitals, social service agencies and childcare centres. However, smaller establishments had either a reduced requirement or no requirement to fulfill the program, even though many new jobs being created are now in small establishments. In the broader public sector, those with 10 to 50 employees had only to inform their employees about the program, conduct a workforce survey, identify barriers and develop a plan. However, they did not have to develop numerical goals, and had only simplified reporting requirements.[22] Similarly, private sector employers with 50 to 100 employees had modified requirements. Broader public sector employers with less than 10 employees and private sector employers with less than 50 employees had no obligations under the Act.[23] Seasonal employees in the agricultural sector are exempted also. Presumably, homeworkers would also not be covered by the Act.

The Act required employers to be guided by the principle of "reasonable progress."[24] This was a very vague term and thus subject to individual interpretation. Critics feared that this standard provided a loophole for employers if an employee complained of a violation of the Act.

The Act did not view "seniority rights" on lay-offs and recall as discriminatory[25] unless a board of inquiry under the Human Rights Code found it to be so. This seemed unnecessarily bureaucratic. It is known that most people of colour and women are the last hired, first laid off and the last called back to work.[26] This is because many of them are in sectors, or work in employment conditions, that marginalize them from the benefits of seniority. For instance, many are in part-time, contract, casual or piece work, which is referred to as "precarious" employment. The hard-earned rights of senior workers is worth preserving, however, if this preservation amounts to systemic discrimination, then should it not be subject to further examination and expansion? This issue is crucial, given current reorganizing schemes being undertaken by both the private and the public sectors. The United Steelworkers of America[27] recognized this need to re-examine seniority rights in its bid to negotiate employment equity plans for First Nations members in its collective agreement with Placer Dome Inc. Among other provisions, the union negotiated that preference will be given to First Nations members in layoffs and recall from lay-offs regardless of seniority.

As mentioned before, the future of the provincial employment equity legislation is uncertain given the fact that Premier Harris has unequivocally denounced it, calling it a "quota system". Some companies are apparently going to continue with their employment equity plans on a voluntary basis because they view them as "good business decisions".[28]

## Community Unionism

Community unionism involves organizing and at the same time building broader community support around workers. The International Ladies Garment Workers' Union (ILGWU) does this with homeworkers in Toronto, predominantly of Chinese, Vietnamese and South Asian backgrounds. The need for community unionism among homeworkers was evident after a research project initiated by the ILGWU in 1991 revealed not only their super-exploitation as pieceworkers but also their extreme social isolation.

Outreach was conducted through community networks and the media, and a Homeworkers Association (HWA) was formed. The HWA organizes social and recreational activities, such as trips and gatherings over tea, educational sessions, legal clinics, counselling and advocacy. It is also part of a larger group called the Coalition for Fair Wages and Working Conditions for Homeworkers. This coalition has lobbied the Ontario government to make changes to the Employment Standards Act in order to ensure fair wages and working conditions for homeworkers. The coalition also launched a "Clean Clothes Campaign" which is designed to raise consumer awareness about the exploitation of homeworkers who may have sewn the garments they are buying. Part of the campaign asks consumers to fill out a "score card" about retailers and lists the benefits of being supplied with or buying garments by manufacturers who do not exploit homeworkers. The campaign urges retailers to get their supplies from manufacturers who pay fair wages and who provide good working conditions.

**Anti-Racism Education**

Anti-racist education is a crucial element of fighting racism, whether it is through legislation, collective agreement or community activity. A very successful example of an educational program is a 10-week course called, "Combatting Racism in the Workplace," also published in book form in 1983. It was developed by staff at the Cross Cultural Communications Centre, a community-based educational resource centre in Toronto, in conjunction with the Centre for Labour Studies at Humber College. The 30-hour course for union activists was piloted as "Work, Racism and Labour", but the curriculum generated out of that has been adapted for a variety of settings over the years.

## Notes

1. Human Rights Committee, Ontario Federation of Labour," Fighting Racial Harassment," Fact Sheet #2, (October, 1993).

2. This estimate was received from the Ontario Federation of Labour during an interview with June Veacock, Human Rights Director of the OFL, Toronto, February 22, 1995.

3. Ronnie Leah, "Linking the Struggles: Racism, Feminism and the Union Movement" in *Race, Class, Gender: Bonds and Barriers,* Jesse Vorst, Das Gupta, Ng et al. (eds.) (Winnipeg: Society for Socialist Studies/Garamond Press 1991). See also my chapter in Vic Satzewich (ed.) *The Racist Imagination,* (Toronto: University of Toronto Press, forthcoming).

4. Ontario Human Rights Commission (OHRC), *Exceptions to the Equality Rights Provisions of the Ontario Human Rights Code, As They Relate to the Workplace* (Ontario: OHRC).

5. Ibid, p.1.

6. Wei Fu, "Human Rights and the Ontario Human Rights Commission," a presentation to the Standing Committee on Government Agencies of the Legislative Assembly of Ontario, 1994.

7. Stan Gray, "Hospitals and Human Rights," *Our Times,* Vol. 13, No. 6, (December, 1994).

8. Wei Fu, "Human Rights."

9. Arnold Minors, "Towards Eliminating Racism From the OHRC: A Report to the Anti-Racism Committee," November, 1992; Donna Young, "The Donna Young Report: The Handling of Race Discrimination Complaints at the OHRC," October 23, 1992.

10. Minors, "Towards Eliminating."

11. Young, "Young Report."

12. Prominent NDP member and author of *The Stephen Lewis Report,* Toronto, (June 9, 1992).

13. Tania Das Gupta, "Working Together: A Case Study, Toronto's South Asian Community," *Diva,* Vol. 1, Issue 2, (July, 1988).

14. "Fired Over Pay Protest Pizza Workers Rehired," *Toronto Star,* (December 15, 1982).

15. Ray Kuszelewski, "Wheels of Justice: The John Persaud Story," *Our Times,* Vol. 10, No. 2, (March, 1991), pp.30-32.

16. *Canadian Human Rights Reporter,* Vol. 6, Decision 445, (May-June 1985).

17. Task Force for Anti-Racism Action Centre, "Proposal to Establish Anti-Racism Action Centre," Toronto, (Summer, 1994).

18. WWIW is an umbrella organization in Toronto of community-based agencies serving immigrant, refugee and women of colour. It emphasizes developing community resources, information sharing, skills development, social action and coalition building. CCCC is a community education and resource centre in Toronto devoted to developing programs and materials on anti-racism, multi-

culturalism, immigration, immigrant women, women of colour, refugees and organizational development. It provides consultations, workshops, courses, publishes and distributes books and houses a library.

19. Abella, *Equality in Employment.*

20. Allan, *Employment Equity*; Catherine Akilah Meade, *Employment Equity For Visible Minority Women. Ontario*: Urban Alliance on Race Relations and Ontario Women's Directorate.

21. Roseanne Bonanno, "Employment Equity Findings Questioned," *Human Rights Reporter*, undated.

22. Ontario Ministry of Citizenship, *Employment Equity in Action: An Overview of Ontario's Employment Equity Regulations*, (June 1994) p.6.

23. Office of the Employment Equity Commissioner, *Getting Ready: Preparing For Ontario's Employment Equity Act.* Ontario: Ministry of Citizenship, 1994, p.4.

24. Office of the Employment Equity Commissioner, *Getting Ready*, p.3.

25. Ontario Ministry of Citizenship, "Employment Equity in Action", p. 12.

26. Allan, *Employment Equity*, p. 19.

27. United Steelworkers of America, "Employment Equity For First Nations Employees", conference proceedings, *Employment Equity: Legal Requirements and Consequences for Unions*, Toronto, November 1994.

28. Kelly Toughhill, "Firms Back Equity," *The Toronto Star*, (June 21, 1995), p. A2.

# Bibliography

Abella, Irving and David Millar. *The Canadian Worker in the Twentieth Century*. Toronto: Oxford University Press, 1978

Abella, Rosalie. *Equality in Employment*. A Commission Report. Ottawa. November, 1984.

Andrew, Allan. "Auditing Race Relations Practices of Metro Police." *Currents*, Vol. 8 (1), June, 1993, p. 14-16.

Allan, Jane. *Employment Equity: How We Can Use It To Fight Workplace Racism*. Toronto: Cross Cultural Communication Centre, 1988.

Angus Reid Group. *Highlights of Attitudes About Multiculturalism and Citizenship*. Canada: Multiculturalism and Citizenship, 1991.

Armstrong, Pat, Hugh Armstrong, Jacqueline Choiniere, Gina Feldberg and Jerry White. *Take Care: Warning Signals for Canada's Health System*. Toronto: Garamond Press, 1994

Armstrong, Pat, Jacqueline Choiniere and, Elaine Day. *Vital Signs: Nursing in Transition*. Toronto: Garamond Press, 1993.

Bannerji, Himani. *Thinking Through: Essays on Feminism, Marxism, and Anti-Racism*. Toronto: Women's Press, 1995.

Bonnano, Roseanne. "Employment Equity Findings Questioned." *Human Rights Reporter*, undated.

Borowoy, Jan and Fanny Yuen. "ILGWU Homeworkers' Study: Summary of Study Findings," Toronto, 1993.

Brand, Dionne and Krisantha Sri Bhaggiyadatta. 1986 *Rivers Have Sources Trees Have Roots: Speaking Of Racism*. Toronto: Cross Cultural Communication Centre.

Brand, Dionne. "Black Women and Work: the Impact of Racially Constructed Gender Roles on the Sexual Division of Labour: Part 1." *Fireweed*, 25, Fall, 1987, p. 28-37.

Brown, Rosemary. "Children and Racism." *Multiculturalism*, Vol. III (2),1979, p. 19-22.

Burawoy, Michael. "Towards A Marxist Theory of the Labour Process. Braverman and Beyond." Politics *and Society*, Vol 8, (3-4), 1978.

Calliste, Agnes. "Canada's Immigration Policy and Domestics from the Caribbean: the Second Domestic Scheme" in Jesse Vorst, Tania Das Gupta, et al (eds.), *Race, Class, Gender: Bonds and Barriers*. Winnipeg: Society for Socialist Studies, 1991.

Calliste, Agnes. "Women of 'Exceptional Merit': Immigration of Caribbean Nurses to Canada." *Canadian Journal of Women and the Law*, Vol. 6 (1), 1993, p. 85-102.

Cameron, Barbara and Teresa Mak. "Working Conditions of Chinese Speaking Homeworkers in the Toronto Garment Industry: Summary of the Results of a Survey Conducted by the ILGWU," Toronto, 1991.

Campbell, Marie. "Management as "Ruling": A Class Phenomenon in Nursing." Studies *in Political Economy*, 27, Autumn, 1988.

Canadian Civil Liberties Association. Letter From A. Alan Borovoy to the Honourable Bob Mackenzie. Toronto. January 18, 1991.

Chan, Anthony B. "Orientalism and Image Making: the Sojourner in Canadian History." *The Journal of Ethnic Studies*, Vol. 9 (3), Fall, 1981 p. 37-46.

Chinese Canadian National Council. *Brief to the Honourable Gregory Sorbara, Minister Responsible For Women's Issues*. March 29, 1988.

City of Toronto. *Equal Opportunity: Detecting Bias: Part One*. Toronto: City of Toronto, 1983.

Cockburn, Cynthia. *Brothers*. London: Pluto Press, 1983.

Cockburn, Cynthia. *Machinery of Dominance: Women, Men and Technical Knowledge*. London: Pluto Press, 1985.

"Come To Henry Fong's Appeal." Unpublished document, Toronto, 1973.

Commission on Systemic Racism on the Ontario Criminal Justice System. *Racism Behind Bars: the Treatment of Black and Other Racial Minority Prisoners in Ontario Prisons*. Ontario: Queen's Printer for Ontario.

Court of Appeal for Ontario. *Between Her Majesty the Queen and Carlton Parks*. October 20, 1992.

Cox, Oliver. *Caste, Class and Race*. New York: Doubleday & Co. Inc., 1948.

Daenzer, Patricia. *Regulating Class Privilege: Immigrant Servants in Canada, 1940s to 1990s*. Toronto: Canadian Scholars' Press, 1993.

Das Gupta, Tania. *Degradation and Deskilling: The Case of the Garment Industry in Toronto*. PhD Thesis, University of Toronto, 1986.

Das Gupta, Tania. "Globalization and Domestication: Two Sides of the Same Coin." Unpublished paper, York University, September, 1994.

Das Gupta, Tania. "Families of Native Peoples, Immigrants and, People of Colour" in Nancy Mandell and Ann Duffy (eds.), *Canadian Families: Diversity, Conflict and Change*. Toronto: Harcourt Brace, 1995.

Canadian Human Rights Reporter. Vol 6, Decision 445, May-June, 1985.

Davis, Angela. *Women, Race and Class*. London: The Women's Press, 1981.

Doris Marshall Institute and Arnold Minors & Associates. Ethno-Racial Equality: A Distant Goal? An Interim Report to Northwestern General Hospital. Toronto, 1994.

Duffy, Andrew. "Blacks Near Ghettos, Study Says." Toronto *Star*, October 7, 1991, p. A1-A7.

Edwards, Richard. *Contested Terrain*. New York: Basic Books Inc., 1979.

Elson, Diane. "Nimble Fingers and Other Fables" in Wendy Chapkis and Cynthia Enloe (eds.), *Of Common Cloth: Women in the Global Textile Industry*. Amsterdam:

Transnational Institute, 1983.

Essed, Philomena. *Everyday racism: Reports From Women of Two Cultures.* California: Hunter House Inc., 1990.

Estable, Alma and Mechthilde Meyer. *A Discussion Paper on Settlement Needs of Immigrant Women in Ontario.* Immigrant Settlement and Adaptation Program, Canada Employment and Immigration Commission, Toronto, March, 1989.

Faber, Seymour. "Working Class Organization." *Our Generation*, Vol. II (2), 1975.

Final Report and Summary of Information Gathered From Service Providers, Residents and Racial Minority Community Organizations in the Jane-Finch Community Regarding the Quality of Police-Minority Community Relations. Unpublished paper. Toronto. January 6, 1989.

Fu, Wei. "Human Rights and the OHRC." A presentation to the Standing Committee on Government Agencies of the Legislative Assembly of Ontario, 1994.

Galt, Virginia. "Chinese Canadians Fight Racism." *Globe and Mail*, April 26, 1991 p. A7.

Game, Ann and Rosemary Pringle. *Gender At Work.* Sydney: George Allen, 1983.

Gannage, Charlene. *Double Day, Double Bind.* Toronto: The Women's Press, 1986.

"The Global Garment Industry: Industrial Model of the Future." *Economic Justice Report*, Vol. V (1), April, 1994.

Gordon, David M., Richard Edwards and Michael Reich. *Segmented Work, Divided Workers.* Cambridge: Cambridge University Press, 1982.

Gray, Stan. "Hospitals and Human Rights." *Our Times*, Vol. 13 (6), December, 1994 p. 17-20.

Hardill, Kathy. "Discovering Fire Where the Smoke Is: Racism in the Healthcare System. *Towards Justice in Health*, Summer, 1993.

Hart, Michael M. *Canadian Economic development and the International Trading System.* Toronto: University of Toronto, 1985.

Head, Wilson. *An Exploratory Study of Attitudes and Perceptions of Minority and Majority Group Healthcare Workers.* Ontario: Ministry of Labour, 1985.

Henry, Frances and Carol Tator. "Fleming's Racism Poll Raises Old Questions With Few Answers." Toronto *Star*, March 31, 1982.

Henry, Frances and Effie Ginzberg. *Who Gets the Work? A Test of Racial Discrimination in Employment.* Toronto: Social Planning Council and Urban Alliance on Race Relations, 1985.

Henry Frances and Effie Ginzberg. *No Discrimination Here? Toronto Employers and the Multiracial Workforce.* Toronto: Social Planning Council and Urban Alliance on Race Relations, 1985.

Herman, Andrew. "Conceptualizing Control: Domination and Hegemony in the Capitalist Labour Process." *The Insurgent Sociologist*, Vol. 11 (3), Fall, 1982.

hooks, bell. *Ain't I A Woman: Black Women and Feminism.* Boston: Southend Press, 1981.

hooks, bell. *Black Looks: Race and Representation.* Toronto: Between the Lines, 1992.

Human Rights Committee, Ontario Federation of Labour. "Fighting Racial Harassment," Fact Sheet # 2, October, 1993.

Institute of Race Relations. *Patterns of Racism, Book 2*. England: Institute of Race Relations, 1982.

International Ladies Garment Workers Union (ILGWU). "General Executive Board Report to the 40th Convention of the ILGWU." June, 1989.

ILGWU. *The Race To the Bottom*. Brief Presented to the Government of Ontario Special Committee on the NAFTA, Toronto, April 8, 1993.

ILGWU. *When One Door Closes... Another One Opens? A Follow-up Study on the Closure of the Great Sewing Exchange*, ILGWU, Toronto, June, 1994

Jain, Harish. "Draft Employment Equity Bill Needs Major Overhaul." *Toronto Star*, August 28, 1993, p. A23.

James, Carl E. *Seeing Ourselves: Exploring Race, Ethnicity and Culture*. Toronto: Thompson Educational Publishing, 1995.

Johnson, Laura C. *The Seam Allowance*. Canada: The Women's Press, 1982.

Jones, Kathy and Valerie Huff. "Plant Closures." Our *Times*, Vol. 8 (1),1989, p.22-25.

Krahn, Harvey and Graham S. Lowe. *Work, Industry and Canadian Society*. Canada: Nelson Canada, 1988.

Kuszelewski, Ray. "Wheels of Justice: the John Persaud Story." *Our Times*, Vol. 10 (2), March, 1991, p. 30-32.

Kwan, Cheuk. "The Anti-W5 Movement" in Barb Thomas and Charles Novogrodsky (eds), *Combatting Racism in the Workplace Readings Kit*. Toronto: Cross Cultural Communication Centre, 1983.

Kwan, Cheuk. "The Foreign Threat That Never Was." *The Asianadian*. Vol. 2 (3), Winter, 1980, p. 21-22.

Leah, Ronnie. 1991 "Linking the Struggles: Racism, Feminism and the Union Movement" in Jesse Vorst, Tania Das Gupta, et al (eds.), *Race, Class, Gender: Bonds and Barriers*. Winnipeg: Society for Socialist Studies, 1991.

Lee, Patricia. "Chinese-Canadian Women: A demographic Profile." Chinese Canadian National Council, Toronto, March, 1992.

Lee-Cunin, Marina. *Daughters of Seacole: A Study of Black Nurses in West Yorkshire*. West Yorkshire: West Yorkshire Low Pay Unit Ltd., 1989.

Lewis, Stephen. *The Stephen Lewis Report*. Toronto, June 9, 1992.

Li, Peter S. *The Chinese in Canada*. Toronto: Oxford University Press. 1988

Lior, Karen. "Briefing Notes: Federal language Training Policy," Toronto, undated.

Lior, Karen. "LINC To What?" *Women's Education des Femme*, Vol. 10 (3-4), Winter, 1993.

Lipsig-Mumme, Carla. "Organizing Women in the Clothing Trades: Homework and the 1983 Garment Strike in Canada." *Studies in Political Economy*, 22, Spring, 1987, p.41-71.

Mackie, Marlene. "Ethnic Stereotype and Prejudice: Alberta Indians, Hutterites and Ukrainians," 1980 in Jay E. Goldstein and Rita M. Bienvenue (eds.), *Ethnic Relations in Canada*. Toronto: Butterworths, 1985.

Mahon, Rianne. "Canadian Labour in the Battle of the Eighties." *Studies in Political Economy*, Summer, 1983.

Makovec, Katerina. "Employment Equity," seminar at York University, Toronto, October 28, 1993.

Marx, Karl. "Preface to a Contribution to the Karl Marx Critique of Political Economy" in Erich Fromm, *Marx's Concept of Man*. New York: Frederick Unger Publishers, 1981.

McDiarmid, Garnet and David Pratt. *Teaching Prejudice*. Toronto: Ontario Institute of Studies in Education, 1967.

McIntosh, Peggy. "White Privilege: Unpacking the Invisible Knapsack." *Peace and Freedom*. July-August, 1989.

Meade, Catherine Akilah. *Employment Equity for Visible Minority Women*. Ontario: Urban Alliance on Race Relations and Ontario Women's Directorate.

Meggs, Geoff. "Quality Caring." *Our Times*, Vol. 14 (2), May/June, 1995.

Minors, Arnold. "Towards Eliminating Racism from the OHRC." A report to the Anti-Racism Committee, November, 1992.

Mitter, Swasti. *Common Fate, Common Bond: Women in the Global Economy*. London: Pluto Press, 1986.

Morgan, Charlotte. "Speaking Out On Racism: An Interview with Enid Lee." *OPSTF News*. April, 1989 p. 6-9.

Multiculturalism and Citizenship Canada. *Multiculturalism: What Is It Really About?* Canada: Ministry of Supply and Services, 1991.

Murray, Maureen. "Blacks Call For Action After Riot in Halifax." *Toronto Star*, July, 1991, p. A1.

Muszynski, Leon and Jeffrey Reitz. "Racial and Ethnic Discrimination in Employment." Working Paper #5, Social Planning Council of Metro Toronto. February, 1982.

Ng, Winnie, Roger Kwan, Mr. Law and Wai Man Lee. "A Chinese Worker's Perspective on Canadian Society" in Council of Chinese Canadians in Ontario, *Effective Citizenship in Canada's Multicultural Society – A Chinese Perspective*. Proceedings of the Intercultural Conference, Toronto, April 8-9, 1978.

Ng, Roxana and Tania Das Gupta. "Nation-Builders? The Captive Labour Force of Non-English-Speaking Immigrant Women." *Canadian Women's Studies*, Vol. 3 (1), 1981 p. 83-89.

Nova Scotia Advisory Group on Race Relations. *Report of the Nova Scotia Advisory Group on Race Relations*. Nova Scotia.

Ocran, Amanda, Jennifer Hyndman and, Natalie Jamieson. *Industrial Homework and Employment Standards: A Community Approach to Visibility and Understanding*. A Brief for Improved Employment Legislation for the Ministry of Women's Equality. Vancouver: The Women and Work Research and Education Society and ILGWU, 1993.

Office of the Employment Equity Commissioner. *Getting Ready: Preparing For Ontario's Employment Equity Act*. Ontario: Ministry of Citizenship, 1994.

Ontario Coalition of Black Trade Unionists (OCBTU), a newsletter, 1987-88.

Ontario Council of Agencies Serving Immigrants. "LINC Community Recommendations." Submission to the Honourable Bernard Valcourt, Minister of Employment and Immigration, June, 1993.

Ontario Federation of Labour. "Statement on Racism Hurts Everyone" in *Racism Hurts Everyone Kit*. November 23-26, 1981.

Ontario Human Rights Commission (OHRC). *The Experience of Visible Minorities in the Work World: the Case of MBA Graduates*. Ontario: Ontario Human Rights Commission, 1983.

Ontario Human Rights Commission Reports.

Ontario Human Rights Commission. *Exceptions To the Equality Rights Provisions of the Ontario Human Rights Code, As They Relate to the Workplace*. Ontario: OHRC.

Ontario Ministry of Citizenship. *Employment Equity in Action: An Overview of Ontario's Employment Equity Regulations*. June, 1994.

Ontario Women's Directorate. *Workplace Harassment: An Action Guide For Women*. Ontario: Ontario Women's Directorate, 1994.

Papp, Leslie and Royson James. "Blacks Still Shut Out of Boardrooms Despite Promise of More Opportunity." *Toronto Star*, January 16, 1989, p. A1.

Pineo, Peter C. "The Social Standing of Ethnic and Racial Groupings", 1980, in Jay E. Goldstein and Rita M. Bienvenue (eds.), *Ethnic Relations in Canada*. Toronto: Butterworths, 1985.

Porter, John. *The Vertical Mosaic*. Toronto: The University of Toronto Press, 1965.

Priest, Lisa. "Hospitals Helping More Group Says." *Toronto Star*, May 18, 1995, p. A34.

Reitz, Jeffrey G. *Ethnicity and Inequality and Segregation in Jobs*. Toronto: University of Toronto, 1981.

Rinehart, James W. *The Tyranny of Work*. Canada: Longman Canada Ltd, 1975.

Said, Edward. *Orientalism*. London: Routledge & Kegan Paul, 1978.

Satzewich, Vic. *The Racist Imagination*. Toronto: University of Toronto, forthcoming.

Scharr, Stuart. "Orientalism At the Service of Imperialism." *Race and Class*, Vol. XXI (1), Summer, 1979, p.67-79.

Scrivener, Leslie. "Fight For Promised Raise Leaves 23 Women Jobless." *Toronto Star*, November 23, 1982, p. D18.

Seward, Shirley B. "Challenges of Labour Adjustment: the Case of Immigrant Women in the Clothing Industry." Studies in Social Policy, Ottawa, March, 1990.

Sharma, Nandita. "Restructuring Society, Restructuring Lives: The Global Restructuring of Capital and Women's Paid Employment in Canada." *Socialist Studies Bulletin*, 37, July-September, 1994.

Siu, Bobby. "The Employment of Indo-Chinese Refugees in Toronto." Paper Presented at Conference of Council of Chinese Canadians in Ontario, Toronto, November 10-11, 1979.

Siu, Bobby. "The Bubble Bursts: the Coming Crises of the Chinese Community." *Asianadian*. Vol 4 (2), July, 1982, p. 2-6.

Smith, Dorothy E. "Feminist Reflections on Political Economy" in M. Patricia Connelly and Pat Armstrong (eds.), *Feminism in Action: Studies in Political Economy*. Toronto: Canadian Scholars' Press, 1992.

Sparks, Corinne. *Women of Colour in the Legal Profession: A Panoply of Multiple Discrimination*. Appendix 10 to the Report of the Canadian Bar Association Task Force on Gender Equality in the Legal Profession. Halifax, Nova Scotia. August, 1993.

Spears, John. "Africville Won't Die, Blacks Vow." *Toronto Star*, July 29, 1991 p.A14.

Stam, Robert. "From Stereotype to Discourse: Methodological Reflexions on Racism in the Media." *Cineaction* 32, Fall, 1993 p. 10-29.

Tabb, William K. "Capitalism, Colonization and Racism." *The Review Of Radical Political Economics*. Vol. 3 (3), Summer, 1971.

Tajima, Renee E. "Lotus Blossoms Don't Bleed: Images of Asian Women" in Asian Women United of California (ed.), *Making Waves: An Anthology of Writings By and About Asian American Women*. Boston: Beacon Press, 1989.

Taskforce for Anti-Racism Action Centre." Proposal to Establish Anti-Racism Action Centre," Toronto, Summer, 1994.

Tatroff, Daniel. "Under the Knife in Chilliwack." *Our Times*, Vol. 14 (2), May/June, 1995.

Thornhill, Esmeralda. "Focus on Black Women" in Jesse Vorst, Tania Das Gupta et al (eds.), *Race, Class, Gender: Bonds and Barriers*. Winnipeg: Society for Socialist Studies, 1991.

Toughhill, Kelly. "Firms Back Equity." *Toronto Star*, June 21, 1995, p. A2.

Tyler, Tracey. "Burning Issue." *Toronto Star*, January 31,1993, p. B1-B8.

U.S. Commission on Civil Rights. "Commercial TV – the Portrayal of Women and Minorities" in *Window Dressing on the Set: Women and Minorities on TV*. August, 1977.

United Steelworkers of America. "Employment Equity for First Nations Employees," Toronto, undated.

Urban Alliance on Race Relations. *The Second Annual Employment Equity Forum of the Urban Alliance on Race Relations, Verbatim Proceedings*. Toronto: Urban Alliance on Race relations, 1990.

Walker, James W. St. G. *Racial Discrimination in Canada: The Black Experience*. Canada: Canadian Historical Association, 1985.

Ward, Peter W. *White Canada Forever*. Montreal: McGill Queen's University Press, 1978.

*Women in Industry: North-South Connections*. Canada: The North-South Institute, 1985.

Wong, Joseph. 1992 "Some Myths About Hong Kong Immigrants." *Toronto Star*, October 15, 1992.

Wong, Shana. 1991 "Issues Facing Asian Canadian Women," Chinese Canadian National Council, Toronto, 1991.

Wotherspoon, Terry (ed.), *The Political Economy of Education*. Toronto: Methuen, 1987.

Wotherspoon, Terry. "The Impact of Healthcare Deinstitutionalization on the Organization and Delivery of Housing Services" in B. Singh Bolaria and Rosemary Bolaria (eds.), *Women, Medicine and Health*. Halifax: Fernwood Publishing, 1994.

Young, Donna. *The Donna Young Report: The Handling of Race Discrimination Complaints At the Ontario Human Rights Commission*, Toronto, October 23, 1992.

Yyelland, Byrad. "Structural Constraints, Emotional Labour and Nursing Work" in B. Singh Bolaria and Rosemary Bolaria (eds.), *Women, Medicine and Health*. Halifax: Fernwood Publishing, 1994.

# Index